In the House of Rising Sounds

In the House of Rising Sounds

A Boisterous Music Bar, a Faith in Transition, and the Thin Space They Inhabited

Stephen Copeland

RESOURCE *Publications* · Eugene, Oregon

IN THE HOUSE OF RISING SOUNDS
A Boisterous Music Bar, a Faith in Transition, and the Thin Space They
Inhabited

Resource Publications
An Imprint of Wipf and Stock Publishers
199 W. 8th Ave., Suite 3
Eugene, OR 97401

www.wipfandstock.com

PAPERBACK ISBN: 978-1-6667-5240-3
HARDCOVER ISBN: 978-1-6667-5241-0
EBOOK ISBN: 978-1-6667-5242-7

03/08/23

To Mom, through whom I first experienced sound.

"In the silence of the afternoon all is present and all is inscrutable in one central tonic note to which every other sound ascends or descends, to which every other meaning aspires, in order to find its true fulfillment. To ask when the note will sound is to lose the afternoon: it has already sounded, and all things now hum with the resonance of its sounding."

—THOMAS MERTON, "DAY OF A STRANGER"

"Everything in the world has a spirit that can be released by its sound."

—OSKAR FISCHINGER TO JOHN CAGE

Contents

Prologue

FROM A PERCUSSIONIST I learned that the drum is our first experience with sound. In the womb the heartbeat of the mother is already forming the baby's ears, inviting them into a life of song and dance. A Native American parable tells how the Maker of the Universe let all creatures roam freely about the earth but first implanted in them a cosmic drumbeat so the curious or lost creatures could *always* find their way back home.

There's a sentence in the thirteenth chapter of John's gospel that is easy to miss. At the Last Supper, we're told that the disciple "whom Jesus loved" reclined at Jesus's side, or, as some translations say, leaned back on his chest. I like to imagine the disciple was listening to Jesus's heartbeat. I like to think the disciple knew he was home.

I used to think faith was all about having the right beliefs and convincing others to believe the same. Now, I think faith—*life*—is more about finding space to listen for that "central tonic note to which every other sound ascends or descends," those reverberations from the core of reality which can feel as intimate as oneness and as disorienting as emptiness.

Prologue

Sometimes, I've learned, there are conduits for these cosmic sounds—everyday places which become sacred space . . . the chests of those who love us, where we can lean back, rest, and be formed by their heart . . . openings in our own hearts where truths rise up to be received, to be *heard*.

This book is an exploration of one of those conduits, a "thin space" between heaven and earth which introduced me to contemplation, where I learned to lean back, rest, put my ear on its beating heart, and listen.

In February 2021, on the heels of finishing the fourth rewrite of this book, I got a call from my dad, who, in a broken voice, told me that he had horrible news. Mom had passed away unexpectedly in her sleep. She was sixty years old with no illnesses or conditions. Just three months before, I had danced and cried with her on my wedding day. It felt as if she had her best days ahead of her, which my wife and I hoped would include fulfilling her dream of being a grandmother. We had our first child right before this book was accepted for publication.

As I write, I find myself in the midst of a different kind of darkness and emptiness, one far different than the panic attacks I write briefly about in this book. It would be inappropriate for me to act or write as if I have any kind of bearing. I cannot tell you it will be okay as I try to trust my own journey through empty landscapes. For the winter I have no pep talk.

Yet I feel it is fitting for this book to be called what it is called. Mom passed down to us her love for musicals, for sound. She taught us to read expressions on faces and the movement on stages and the rising lyrics from dream-filled eyes. Having held and carried us—in her womb and in her loving arms and on all those van rides as she surrendered us to the world—she taught us to do the same with sound: to trust what is rising within, especially if it could help someone else, and sing that good news with all our might.

A couple days before Mom passed away, Dad said he heard her scream in the kitchen. He rushed in and exclaimed, "Kim, are you okay?"

But when he saw her, there was no sign of trouble.

"Yeah," she smiled, "I just yelled 'Sprinkles!'"

She was dancing and singing to one of her favorite GEICO commercials.

This book is for her. I hope these songs remind you to come alive on the dance floor of your life. As my mentor once said to me, "That's what Love can do, it can free you to be unashamedly yourself." That was one of the many gifts Mom gave to me.

It was my mother's heart that somehow stopped that fateful February morning, but I will be forever seeking to align my heart with hers, as I follow her drumbeat, the purest sound I've heard, back home.

1

That's What Love Can Do

A CANDLE BURNED BETWEEN us in a small, dim conference room.

"Have you ever been to the Double Door Inn?" my mentor asked.

I drew a blank. "Uh, is that a new brewery?"

Here in Charlotte, North Carolina, breweries and condominiums were multiplying like bacteria.

Dave laughed. "Monday nights at the Double Door: best live music you'll ever hear," he exclaimed.

I didn't know there was live music in Charlotte. I hadn't even heard of any kind of art in this banking town, pulsating with the American Dream, erecting its slick, modern buildings atop its culture and history, its citizen-workers in suits and ties chasing, always chasing, the "bottom line."

That was before I discovered that a robust art scene hummed in the shadows of the city's corporate facade. To me, Charlotte lacked character, culture, and identity, blinded by the glare of its own shine. But that was before I found the Double Door Inn, or, better said, before the Double Door Inn found me.

Dave blew out the candle and stood up. "Grab your hoodie and let's go!"

I met Dave a year or so before when he noticed a disheveled writer (me) fumbling through a big binder of transcribed interviews in a coffeeshop. Apparently my own confused, disorderly vibe comforted him that I could be trusted with his own creative chaos. He asked me to help him on his book about union with God,[1] but really, every time we got together, Dave was helping me reconstruct my broken faith. Dave was a mystic. I had never before encountered a *Christian* whose faith was so open, inclusive, and cosmic. Dave's spirituality was in stark contrast to the religion I had been immersed in but could no longer sustain: highly dualistic divisions between sacred and secular, saved and unsaved. Those stark contrasts birthed a worldview of certitude in which those who believed were right and those who disagreed with them were wrong, and just about everything had a black-or-white answer.

Each time Dave and I met, he would light a candle. The flame, he told me, served as a reminder of God's presence—here, now, in us, through us. The spiritual life, he said, was about becoming more aware of what was already true. The same awareness we had for the candle—the flickering light on the walls around us and the tobacco scent that permeated the room—could extend to the deepest spiritual mysteries in life.

Before I met Dave, a candle was just a candle.

When Dave and I arrived at the Double Door Inn, we parked next to a strip of struggling restaurants. Nothing around us looked like a music venue—more like we were picking up Chinese take-out. I looked at him and asked, "Where the hell are we?"

He smiled.

When he guided me next door to an old, white, battered house, I wondered if I had gotten this Dave guy all wrong. Maybe this strange house was where he massacred his victims, chopping them up and eating them in a stew. But as we drew closer, I could hear music percolating through the walls, and I felt relief that my mentor was not a sociopathic cannibal and I would indeed live to see another day.

We paid five dollars cash at the door and walked into that shack of a thing. Inside, it looked just as inconspicuous and run-down as it did from the outside. I had been to small music clubs before, but this place was *tiny*. There were barely a dozen stools at the bar. The chairs facing the stage were odd wooden theater seats bolted into a platform on the floor. In the back of the bar was a pool table, an arcade machine, and a smelly bathroom. Upstairs was a small green room for the bands.

Hanging on the walls around the establishment were dozens of black-and-white photos of musicians who had played there, as patrons brought them their stories and love for music. There was nothing "sexy" about this place. But as the music filled the white house, and as people filled the music, I was seized by a sense of belonging there—a place of inner contentment in a world that only reinforces our discontent, convincing us of our incompleteness. As Dave and I sat in the back row of those strange, uncomfortable wooden seats, I finally began to understand why Dave always lit a candle.

For the next two hours, I took in the scene as the six-person jam band that evening called the Monday Night Allstars performed anything from blues to funk to soul to R&B—their talent evident, their joy even more evident—as they played their hearts out, inviting all in attendance to come as they were and enter into the experience that was their music. It was as if I had stepped behind the veil of that corporate city in the Bible Belt—shrouded with all its glamorous, sanctimonious facades—and had found something that was real, a place where all that mattered was love and joy, a place where nobody really gave a shit, a place where nobody masked their emptiness by "doing" and instead willingly entered into "being."

Sitting there in that uncomfortable seat, absorbed by the sounds, I felt connected to the depth and beauty of life. I left behind all my overthinking about nothing. In this city where we were always going, doing, accomplishing, pursuing, claiming, attaining . . . now, nothing mattered but the present. The band was swimming in the stream of their collective joy and love-rooted creativity, which freed us to swim along as well, without a care in the world where we were going, because all that mattered was that the water refreshed us and it felt good to swim and we were being carried somewhere. I felt as if I had tasted what I was looking for, something that really was authentic, something true beneath all things.

At one point, Dave nudged me and pointed toward a figure in the crowd—a heavyset man in big glasses and suspenders who was sporting a wide grin and whose head bounced around violently to the beat of the music, perhaps the most unnatural, beautiful, freeing form of dancing I had ever seen.

"That's what Love can do," Dave said to me, eyeing the man with the bouncing head. "It can free you to be unashamedly yourself without a care in the world what others think of you because your reality is Love itself."

That first night at the Double Door was an experience of a contemplative kind of seeing—clear spiritual vision that pierces through the layers of perception, performance, ego, and attachments that cloud our reality and prohibit us from living fully and freely, or, as Jesus said, abundantly. What is this sensation, exactly? What does it teach us about ourselves and Reality? And what do we do when it's gone? For five bucks at the door, I'd gotten a glimpse of a spiritual search worth taking on.

2

Everyday Places, Sacred Spaces

ANCIENT CELTS SAW "THIN places" where heaven and earth come strangely close to touching. I think of it as my feet on the ground, my soul in the stars.

On a trip to Paraguay, I had the opportunity to visit Iguazu Falls across the border in Brazil. Traveling has a way of shaking you from your routine and releasing you from the grip of machine-like doing. Being away can make you question if you were ever really home. I can still taste the water, that rushing mist enveloping us as we stood in the throat of one of the world's wonders. From our vantage point on an outstretched plank, we could see a rainbow rising up out of the gulley as if extending its hand, inviting us to partner with the mystery. I can still hear the waterfalls' beautiful benediction to me: keep walking, keep going, far beyond the walls of certitude my ego had constructed. It was a fitting thing for the Falls to say to me because that's what water naturally does—it moves—and that's what thin places seem to do: they stir us from the inside-out, until our soul is once again animating our hands and our feet and our hearts and our minds.

In the House of Rising Sounds

When Dave initiated me, I was living in the wealthy south side of Charlotte, ironic for a poor writer working at a niche faith-based sports magazine, washing golf carts on weekends to pay my bills. My roommate and I were renting a condominium for a cheap price thanks to missionaries in China who wanted a couple of "good Christian guys" to take care of their belongings, which we were by worldly standards if not by their conservative views. And so I would routinely head uptown to get away from that community in which I did not belong, often to catch a show at the Double Door Inn—usually on a Monday night to watch the Allstars or occasionally on a Tuesday to catch Bill Hanna's weekly jazz band. I often went alone, craving a sound underneath the cacophony of the world.

Each time I went, I glimpsed a reality that I always knew, deep down, was true: we're all more connected than we've dared to imagine. As I've heard it said, "We are not human beings having a spiritual experience; we are spiritual beings having a human experience."[2] Beauty was a deep river that flowed not only through Sunday services and prayer and scripture—all those things I had deemed "spiritual"—but coursed evermore through spaces I least expected: passing conversations, afternoon rain showers, and old white houses.

It was rare that I could convince a Charlotte friend to step into that ramshackle house, especially so late on a Monday, but whenever I had out-of-town visitors I was sure to take them, convinced it was the best gift I could offer them for their Charlotte experience. Plus, I could afford two five-dollar tickets, no problem.

One Monday, just a couple days after New Year's, I took my sister, visiting from our Indianapolis hometown. I think she was just as skeptical when we parked at the Chinese restaurant and walked into the century-old house. She, too, might have been wondering whether Charlotte had turned me into a cannibalistic sociopath. She was even more bemused when we walked in and the place was practically empty, the quietest I'd ever seen it, probably because of the holidays. Fifteen people max, employees included—versus other nights when seventy or eighty people were jam-packed into that space—crowded around the bar, sitting in those quirky seats, but more than anything, turning those wooden, creaky floors into a holy ground for dancing. Tonight, it felt as if we had stumbled into an abandoned bar in some rural Hoosier town.

My sister and I grabbed a beer and a whiskey and sat down in front of an empty, hardly-elevated stage. It was well after ten o'clock when the Monday Night Allstars began to play, traditionally late. But they played with a fervor and enthusiasm as if they were entertaining a sold-out show at Red Rocks instead of a dozen people. The Allstars were lost in the moment, in the music they were creating. And we, too, were lost in their moment, as if we had our favorite band at Red Rocks all to ourselves.

Saxophonist Ziad, in his backwards cap and black-frame glasses, fingers racing at an incomprehensible pace, would often look at his bandmates in awe during their solos, lost in their contribution to the flow.

Lead singer Shana, a curly-haired blonde with a mighty, angelic voice radiating with joy, would often venture off stage in the middle of a song just to hug people in the audience. (Later I would learn this was a nod to tradition, begun by her predecessor, the late great Charles Hairston.)

On the congas was Jim, an older man of Cherokee descent with a gentle smile, his long white hair pulled back in a ponytail, whose eyes would often water while they all swam in the creative river of a song together.

The band's soul flare comprised three African-American men whose families had endured the prejudiced south throughout the sixties and seventies. Rick would calmly pluck away on bass, sometimes stepping up to his microphone to sing an entire song in his low, deep, full, soothing voice. In back-center stage Chris played his drums with a smile, his tenor tone occasionally adding texture to Shana's and Rick's. Joe stood in the corner with his electric guitar, perhaps the most talented yet also the calmest of them all.

When he burst into magnificent solos he remained still as a statue, no need for showmanship, smiling serenely when the crowd went wild as if to say politely, "Thank you for listening."

The raggedy crowd that night was more diverse than a college-admissions advertisement. There was a tall, long-legged cowboy in leather boots, grinning from ear-to-ear as he whooped and hollered during solos. One woman booty-danced alone at the front of the stage, as if at a hip-hop concert. A small group of young professionals crowded around the bar. Behind us sat an elderly couple, perhaps returning to a place they had enjoyed together for decades. And of course there he was again, the heavyset man in suspenders allowing his head to bounce violently around however it pleased, his face radiating joy.

The Allstars made no comments that evening about the shoddy attendance. The only money-related comment was Ziad's usual, "Don't forget to tip your bartenders."

Of course every musician wants to play a sold-out show, but the Allstars didn't look the slightest bit disappointed. They seemed to treat that night as an opportunity to do what they loved: make music for the people who showed up, just as they did every Monday. In fact, the intimacy of the evening might have fueled them all the more. They sweated their asses off that wintry night, exchanging looks with a certain glimmer and excitement as if they were the first human fire-starters.

Before we left that evening, between the All-Stars' first and second sets, I approached the percussionist, looked deep into his eyes past the wrinkles on his face, and said, "Thank you for tonight, this is the closest thing to church I've ever experienced."

He smiled and said, "I know."

Dave had gotten me onto more than one journey: a contemplative, mystical spiritual path and a love affair with the Double-Door Inn, both of which seemed intertwined.

For the next few years my spiritual path felt like traveling out of the orderly city I had constructed—where its citizens were mostly the same, carrying their God around in a Bible, and all the buildings were carefully planned, built upon the foundation of certitude—into the wilderness. All my doubts and bitterness and deconstruction as a city-dweller had spit me out into the open field of mysticism, for lack of a better term. Here, a wonderful dance with all types of people was unfolding. I suppose you could have called my previous home "Doctrine," or perhaps "Certainty," and my new home "Transformation," or perhaps "Mystery." This is the absolute worst thing, yet also the best thing, about a spiritual journey: it changes everything from the inside out, which forces you to approach your exterior world with a brand-new set of eyes, as if you are a stranger to it. At the Double Door Inn I never felt like a stranger—or, if I did, I was united with everyone else in our strangeness.

I was also in the process, consequently, of quitting my dream job at the faith-based sports magazine: the co-workers I loved, the lifestyle of magazine journalism I adored—deadlines and all—and a storytelling outlet I had long enjoyed. Prior to the Supreme Court ruling on same-sex marriage, I'd stirred up trouble by writing a column about a gay Christian soccer player, praising his vibrant faith. Donors kept sending me books about homosexuality. I had poked the bear. Our subscribers deserved better than a subversive in their midst, pushing his own boundaries at the expense of their distress. It wasn't that I was no longer a Christian—it's just that I could no longer be certain about everything. I couldn't be the kind of Christian I felt expected to be.

I went to the Double Door on and off during those years, as I moved out of the missionaries' house in the wealthy Charlotte suburb into the city's grungy arts district. It was my own silly outward declaration of "authenticity," where gunshots sometimes echoed in the night and the homeless charged their phones on my porch. (I was pursuing authenticity the way Don Quixote was restoring chivalry. Apparently, authenticity required a $49.95 a month security system.) It was a fifteen-minute bike ride to the Double Door, so I knew I could get there whenever I wanted. I had plenty of time, I figured, to explore the city.

There were many days when I doubted the decisions I had made. The thing no one tells you about freelancing is the shadow of self-doubt accompanying your every movement. One literary agent I spoke to implied I had thrown my career down the drain by leaving the magazine. He very well may have been right. Who was I without a "platform"?

But every time I thought about my experiences at the Double Door Inn—where the noise of the world slipped away and something different rose up within me and around me—I couldn't help but feel like I was on the right path. I was trying to make decisions based off soul rather than ego, in where my spiritual journey had taken me rather than what it could do for me, on qualitative spiritual experience rather than quantitative worldly benefits.

In journalism school I learned to pursue the truth no matter if it was inconvenient, no matter if it went against personal biases and beliefs, no matter what. My soul, I felt, was on the beat. The deeper it went, the messier the story seemed to get, yet I trusted it was getting closer to the truth. I couldn't get a damned thing published but tried to keep writing, often thinking about the All-stars' declaration before that stifled crowd years before. I stopped going to church, but I lit candles. I had no idea where my life was heading, but I occasionally stumbled into the Double Door Inn, my soul both nourished and convicted to venture deeper.

3

Learning How to Be a Horse Again

I THINK DAVE TOOK me to the Double Door because he sensed that I needed an encounter with something that was true, or, in today's lingo, authentic, that far overused word often spoken by young people in my generation who equate it with airing their dirty laundry on social media to chase likes. Authenticity, I think, is being animated by the truest parts of one's soul, the fullness of the heart—unhindered by the worldly attachments our egos cling to in order to convince ourselves we are whole.

True authentic soul movement brings us deeper into an awareness of our original essence, who we were born to be, what we were made to do, so that we are no longer running in circles locked within our own inner prisons. As trainer Tom Smith said of Seabiscuit, "I just can't help feeling they got him so screwed up running in a circle, he's forgotten what he was born to do. He just needs to learn how to be a horse again."

Art can often break the circular patterns of our lives that ultimately lead us nowhere, dropping us into the open field and daring us to run, as we become wild horses again, as we become who we already are. People didn't seem to run in circles at the Double Door Inn, thinking they were going somewhere. Everyone ran freely through an open field with no destination in mind, for joy was already in their midst. "We rose and came to the field," wrote the great poet Robert Lax in "The Circus of the Sun."[3]

As I ran loose outside the racetracks of religious diligence and professional accomplishment, I thought a lot about why the Double Door Inn felt like such a thin place. It seemed to attract authentic bands and authentic people, who met and joined together like a sudden confluence of stars, a wondrous phenomenon. I began feeling the familiar pull to Inspiration, to give voice to the thinness of this place. I longed to talk to ownership, to the Allstars, to the jazz band, to the bartenders, to the man with the bouncing head. I longed to uncover how this otherworldly gem carried something that was missing in this world that felt so full of shit.

I learned that this strange, dilapidated house—constructed in 1911 as a family residence on a gravel road—had been a blues mecca, especially throughout the seventies and eighties, a must-stop in the southeast for touring blues bands as they made their way from Austin, Texas, to Boston, Massachusetts. It was the "oldest live music venue east of the Mississippi" and the "oldest blues club in the U.S. under original ownership." How had I never heard of the Double Door before Dave?

In June 1982, Eric Clapton played on its stage. Hundreds of other notables had played there, too—Stevie Ray Vaughan, Tom Jones, Delbert McClinton, Gatemouth Brown, JJ Cale, Buddy Guy, Keb' Mo'—along with the annual staples such as the Dixie Dregs and Nighthawks. There was the time Levon Helm rocked out with The Barn Burners and Junior Walker played "Shotgun." Or the time that Drive-By Truckers and Slobberbone played a show together and a bass player memorably hung from the rafters over the stage. Even the modern folk band, the Avett Brothers, recorded their first album at the Double Door and played there several times when they were coming up. Dallas Mavericks owner Mark Cuban and future Hall of Famer Dirk Nowitzki once enjoyed a Monday show at the Double Door. AC/DC guitarist Angus Young visited while on tour to listen to music, and in 2006 Hootie & The Blowfish made a surprise appearance. The list goes on.

One spring morning, as I lay in bed wasting time on my phone, a headline flashed across my screen:

*Central Piedmont Community College in talks
to buy Double Door Inn property in Charlotte*

I clicked on the *Charlotte Observer* article. Was it true? I had assumed the Double Door Inn would be around forever. After forty-three years, why was this blues mecca coming to a close now?

I had to find the owner of the Double Door Inn.

His name, the article said, was Nick Karres. I contacted the *Observer* reporter to get an email for Nick Karres. She responded within minutes.

I emailed Nick. He responded within minutes. *Drop by on a Tuesday or a Thursday at around eleven thirty in the morning*, he said.

I was there on Tuesday.

I parked in the side lot next to that timeless white house and began aimlessly walking around the back of the building. *Come through the back door*, he'd said. I walked up a back ramp to the patio and knocked on the door. No answer. Knocked again, no answer. Wondering where the heck this door might be, I pulled up Nick's email once more on my phone.

Don't use the back ramp, it said.

Finally I found the stupid thing, hidden in a little alleyway on the other side of the patio. I knocked again.

Once again, no answer.

I tried again, this time with a metal door knocker.

"Hello? Who is that?" grunted a muffled voice on the other side.

"Is that you, Nick?" I asked. "It's me, Stephen."

The door opened, and I was greeted by an older, big-boned man with bushy white eyebrows and thin gray hair. In baggy pants and a disheveled shirt, he looked like a movie extra from *Zorba the Greek.*

Nick's demeanor was slightly confused, like he didn't know where he was or why I was there, but he did smile when he gently shook my hand, his eyes falling back down to the floor. As we talked briefly there in the dark, unorganized storage room—surrounded by shelves of Heineken and Yuengling and Land Shark, none of that fancy craft beer Charlotte is known for, the liquid gold that always seemed to drain my bank account—I saw him as a reflection of the establishment he owned: nothing flashy, but welcoming and intriguing. As I followed him out of the room a cat looked at me and meowed.

We walked out into the main area where the bar and the stage were located.

"Well, take a seat," he said to me.

"Is it true?" I asked, almost immediately.

Nick sighed. "It is."

The Double Door Inn would be closing at the turn of the year, he told me. The commercial development in the area as well as the growth of the nearby community college had steadily reduced their parking over the years. How can a music venue survive without parking? Nick said he felt the time had come to let the Double Door Inn go.

Then and there, I knew my time had come as well. It was now or never to explore this thin space—that portal to truth—where authenticity and love and interconnectedness rose up in the form of sound.

It is one thing to leave home. It is another to awaken to the true home that is yourself. In the former, the hero's journey, you go on a search to find yourself; you board the ship and go on the voyage. That had led me to Charlotte. In the contemplative journey, you realize you embody belonging already, just as you are, and therefore must seek to see what is true, at the core of reality, then respond to that truth. My hero's journey had begun with ego. That wasn't a bad thing, but I'd thought it was the elevator I would be taking all the way up to the penthouse before realizing it's more interesting to go down, deep into the soul, because there's an arcade bar in the basement. Or a Double Door Inn.

4

The Evolving House

AT SIXTY-SEVEN, NICK KARRES had a safe, grandfatherly vibe about him that made me feel I could be myself in his presence. He was soft-spoken and humble. He also had a quirkiness about him reminiscent of the "mad scientist" trope. With his big, baggy eyes and his gray hair statically sticking out around the brim of his balding head, a look of oblivion on his face, he would answer my questions in the oddest of fashions—jumping around from thought to thought, interrupting himself in the middle of sentences, leaving me wondering where he was going, but then always, somehow, answering the question I had originally asked. But his very quirkiness made me feel more comfortable. Like the Double Door Inn, I could tell Nick had little interest in coming across as polished—he didn't care to impress me. He was simply himself, which invited me to be myself.

My questioning forced Nick to sit with the reality that the Double Door was really closing, and he spiraled into a reflective state.

Back in the early seventies, he was trying to figure out his life. While working for a local real estate company, he was tasked with leasing the old white house in Elizabeth at 218 Independence Boulevard after the Peggy Houston Lamp Shop relocated. After several business deals fell through due to high interest rates, Nick considered opening a bar in the building—not a music venue, just a bar. He begged his brother Matt to go into business with him. It was a hard sell—a bar in the Bible Belt, controversial at the time—but Matt agreed. Nick's mother came up with the name "Double Door" because the old house had two front doors.

A year into their business venture, the Karres brothers indulged a patron who wanted to play live music and let him set up in the back room. For a quarter, people could go into the back room, sit on the floor, and listen to live music. This arrangement continued for some time, attracting many other local musicians.

Then the music found its way to the front, which became a stage. And one night, thanks to a strand of random encounters, the nationally-acclaimed rock band Dixie Dregs filled the Double Door Inn with sound. That night changed everything. Nick realized the house in Elizabeth he had transformed into a neighborhood bar needed to evolve into a music bar. It was as if, since 1911, the house had been pregnant with music. It took sixty-three years, but once the music was born there was no looking back.

The Dixie Dregs loved playing the Double Door Inn so much—because of its character, natural propensity to hold and carry sound, and the patrons—that they told their friends and tour-mates about the unassuming house in Charlotte. One night blues-rock band the Nighthawks stepped into the old house that didn't look like much from the outside or on the inside, for that matter. But it took only one gig for them to decide not to kill their tour manager and adopt it as a must-stop on the road.

It didn't take long for word to get around, for others to understand what the Dixie Dregs and Nighthawks understood. As I sat with Nick, I couldn't help but wonder if bands liked the Double Door so much not only because of the venue and patrons, but because of Nick Karres. Maybe his gentleness and his adoration for the arts made them feel how he made *me* feel, allowing their creativity to flourish in the space carved out by his contagious passion.

Whenever we get a glimpse of our true essence, the only natural response, as stewards of this life we've been gifted, is to multiply what we have received. At a time when most bars in Charlotte were booking top-forty bands, the Double Door was expanding Charlotte's live-music scene by becoming a primary blues venues in the southeast. The first time Stevie Ray Vaughan played there, six people attended; the second time, thirty; by the third and final time, over a hundred jam-packed the house.

The Double Door became a place for touring blues bands to try new things and evolve, but also to come home. All because Nick was willing to explore the path that mysteriously lit up before him in the early seventies, winding his way through unknown territory into the freedom of his found vocation—service to a community he loved.

It had not been easy managing the place, Nick told me. Excitement over blues, soul, and jazz began to fade in the late nineties, and two decades into its existence, the Double Door was struggling. Charlotte's corporate growth, the development of other areas for night life, the suppression of the arts, the expansion of a nearby community college, and the country's economic crash in 2008 didn't help.

Nick had to make changes to survive. But he could not untaste what he had tasted or un-hear what he had heard. So he kept at it: providing an outlet for blues, jazz, and soul artists to be true to themselves and for those who heard it to be stirred from within. Nick never wandered from cultivating the evolving house's true essence—for the beautiful fringes of the music industry to thrive.

As I learned from Nick the history of the Double Door, I was inspired by how that little house became what it was always supposed to become, how it never stopped changing and evolving.

From a house to a bar.

From a bar to a venue.

From a venue to a landmark.

And now from a landmark to what would soon be dust.

Evolution had found that little white house, and Nick had brought forth his dream. Who knows, maybe once the news was public about the demise of the Double Door Nick was confronting the weight of good-bye. Its dust would mark a thin space, but it wouldn't negate the life that flourished there. That life would go on in everyone who experienced it.

From dust to dust, I like to think that each of us is an evolving house from which beautiful music is meant to arise. We confront sound-proof barriers—whether thrust upon us or of our own making—that block, absorb, or stifle the sound rising from our core. These silencers feed us the lie that the music we are making doesn't belong.

When we believe the lie, we don't realize that we can do the hard work to tear down these soundproof barriers. We stop evolving, and before we know it, we are just a house, static and still. We lose touch with who we are because the truest music of the soul has been silenced.

These silencers can come in the form of systems, stories, ideas, doubts, fears, or people. Many times I've had to confront the bitter truth that *I* am the silencer within my own evolving house, in denial of the drenching mystery, for it would simply demand too much of me—to trust my story, my journey, and therefore myself. Fred Rogers said in an interview that appeared in the remarkable documentary, *Won't You Be My Neighbor?*, "I think those who try to make you feel less than you are—that's the greatest evil." So many times I am the culprit who is making myself feel "less than," negating the inherent dignity and potential of my evolving house.

Can we hear the invitation to become who we are supposed to become? Do we listen for the sounds awakening us to who we are and whose we are? Will we respond to the call, in the words of Paul Tillich, to "accept [our] own acceptance," which is to trust that we are indeed pregnant with music, made by Love and pulsing with love, transcending the need for worldly validation?

5

Powerful Music #1

"So what do you play?" I asked Nick, a couple of hours into our interview.

He looked at me as if I asked him if he'd ever been to the moon.

"I don't play anything, I just like music."

If he had any musical talent at all, he said, it was his ears. He remembered as a kid riding along in his father's 1957 Dodge down Charlotte's winding, tree-tunneled streets as his dad controlled the radio. Whenever a good song came on his old man would turn up the dial and say, "That's a powerful piece of music."

For four decades this had been Nick's driving factor: turning up the dial so others could hear powerful music. Now he had eight months to do what he had always done: give people a taste of something real and true through the gift of an authentic space and honest music—*powerful music.*

Nick offered me a beer, as if to say, "Let's keep talking a while longer."

Never one to turn down a beer, especially after noon (a silly rule people have to convince themselves they don't have drinking problems), I accepted.

Two weekly local acts emerged after the Double Door began to struggle, he told me: the Monday Night Allstars and Tuesday's jazz musician Bill Hanna.

The Monday Night Allstars, Nick explained, were composed of local musicians who each practiced music in his or her respective instrument in full-time capacity. They formed in 1994 and, though some of its members changed, were still playing together each Monday.

I learned that their original lead singer—a big African-American man with an angelic voice, Charles Hairston—passed away in 2009. Whenever Charles showed up at the Double Door Inn on Mondays, albeit always late, his loving presence illuminated the room from the stage, and then sometimes off the stage as he would routinely quiet the band, walk through the crowd, and sing without a microphone.

"He would come right through here," Nick said to me, pointing behind us.

I could see in Nick's eyes that he was trapped in a memory.

He began to tear up.

"I'm sorry," he said, "I never do this."

He paused.

"I miss him."

Charles Hairston, I could tell, sang what Nick believed was the most powerful music of all.

Before I left that afternoon, Nick gave me a thin book about the history of the Double Door by Debby Wallace, a DVD titled "The Legendary Charles Hairston," and a CD of songs that were mostly recorded there in the evolving house.

Scribbled on the CD in sharpie was this: "PM #1."

Powerful Music #1.

6

"Rain Is a Festival"

I WAS HOPING THAT someone would save the Double Door. Its looming closing was yet another blow to the Charlotte music scene. The year before, Southend's Tremont Music Hall, which *Charlotte Magazine* called "the last dirty rock club," closed its doors after twenty years to make room for development (now the area is filled with condos and apartments). That same year, NoDa's beloved Chop Shop closed to clear space for a seven-acre mixed-use development. A couple months after news broke about the Double Door Inn, Amos Southend announced it would be closing after twenty-seven years because surrounding offices, shops, and apartments had swallowed up its parking (Amos would reopen two years later at half-capacity in a smaller part of the building). Someone would later tell me the Double Door was only six years away from being considered for the National Register of Historic Places, which may have positioned it to remain protected and receive grants.

Visit a place like Wilmington or Asheville and you'll find old buildings preserved and repurposed. Some Charlotte neighborhoods like NoDa and Plaza Midwood have successfully repurposed old mills, but Charlotte has gained a reputation for flattening history and erecting towers that glitter (which are ironically more shallow). With one hundred people per day moving to this buzzing city situated between the mountains and the beach, with a booming tech industry and established banking center—the excitement of growth and development continues to trump culture.

I remembered having coffee with a local politician who served on Charlotte's city council. He told me that Charlotte has long been obsessed with becoming a "world class city." He compared Charlotte to a teen on the brink of adulthood: ambitious and bold yet plagued by insecurity, yet to find its identity. He said that if we wanted to do big things for our community, it would take uncovering our lost identity so that our culture could shine brighter than our buildings.

Yet Charlotte is not unlike many American cities and many American people. Compassionate capitalism ought to cultivate art, culture, and history with a generational eye on the future, not just today's "bottom line." But unfettered capitalism seems embedded in American DNA. Nighthawks co-founder Jimmy Thackery would later tell me over the phone, "That's the tragic thing about the Double Door closing: that the thing that was worth the money was the real estate under the building, not what happened inside of it. That's what should be worth a million dollars: what happened inside of it."

Trappist monk Thomas Merton once wrote, "There are some men for whom a tree has no reality until they think of cutting it down."[4] When I was on a performance-treadmill—in my faith, in my career, running tirelessly but going nowhere—Dave gently told me I was valuing the wrong things. I was elevating my spiritual checklist in an attempt to quantify my "closeness" to God. I was elevating my list of professional goals in an attempt to quantify my success as a writer. Union with God was an exploration of what was *already* true, Dave told me.

This understanding was less quantifiable—more abstract for my linear, western, goal-oriented mind—but the shift from *doing* to *being* helped reorient my faith toward what was happening on the *inside*: in my heart, in my mind, in my soul. Was I allowing my awareness of divine oneness—of light—to permeate those dark, forlorn rooms in what St. Teresa of Avila calls the interior castle?[5] Was I allowing what was already true to permeate the areas in my life where I was telling myself lies? When my writing was rejected, did that lead me to reject myself or rest in who I was and whose I was amidst the very real pain and confusion I was experiencing? Whereas the world tended to fling me onto the performance treadmill, at the Double Door Inn I always seemed to have an encounter with what was already true. The depth and beauty of life was to be intimately experienced and received—here, now—as sound overflowed into my reality. What helped me detach from whatever I was using to convince myself of my worth was contemplation, the awakening to who I already am—guided by silence, solitude, or stillness, which often flourishes in thin spaces.

Still, I tended to label things in my life as success or failure based on measurements. The silencers in my evolving house imposed on my life a utilitarian filter. They told me to use the faith-based sports magazine for my own personal benefit even if I no longer belonged there; to use religion not to propel me forward into a deeper transformative journey but rather remain in a place that would be comfortable; to justify all this with the number of articles published each year, the number of retweets on a column, the number of followers on social media I gained, the comforts of a salary. Commodification always seems to emphasize numbers. Leaving that behind was a declaration of a new set of values, that I no longer needed to commodify to justify my purpose.

Commodification is one of the greatest silencers in our evolving houses because it rips soul out of the process and replaces curiosity with judgment. When I give into it, I am no better than Charlotte letting their iconic venues get pummeled.

I just have less money.

Thomas Merton once wrote a beautiful essay titled "Rain and the Rhinoceros," where, in the spirit of Thoreau, he meditated upon the sounds of a rainstorm from his hermitage at the Abbey of Gethsemani in the quiet hills of Kentucky.

"Let me say this before rain becomes a utility that they can plan and distribute for money," Merton wrote. "By 'they' I mean the people who cannot understand that rain is a festival, who do not appreciate its gratuity, who think that what has no price has no value, that what cannot be sold is not real, so that the only way to make something actual is to place it on the market. The time will come when they will sell you even your rain. At the moment it is still free, and I am in it. I celebrate its gratuity and its meaninglessness."[6]

After visiting Iguazu Falls, I found myself on the bus ride back to Asunción, Paraguay, trying to extract some kind of meaning from the experience. Maybe the Falls were telling me to leave my job . . . or to leave Evangelicalism . . . or to commit to singleness. Maybe my experience at the Falls was the perfect ending to my unpublished memoir. In this western mental masturbation of meaning-making, I was filtering my experience through a horizontal, linear lens (what exactly were the Falls telling me, where exactly were they propelling me, and how could I leverage this experience?) rather than a vertical lens (love, union, beauty, contemplation), which perhaps had no "practical" purpose.

Now, I realized, encountering the Falls had been a gratuitous gift. Yes, it was infinitely valuable but perhaps meaningless by my "what is the benefit" standards. Sometimes we are meant not to capture the moment but simply to gaze upon it with wonder, like laying down a net to watch a butterfly fluttering through the air—one day, perhaps, to migrate thousands of miles. Attempts to capture the moment may suffocate its mystery.

"Baptism" was the best word I could find to describe my experience at Iguazu. I was drenched by an intimate presence of Something I could not explain yet felt compelled to explain anyway. Philosopher Peter Rollins said it perfectly, "That which we cannot speak of is the one thing about whom and to whom we must never stop speaking."[7] I once wrote a parable about a mystic who spent each day writing about God but then burned her words in a bonfire at night.

On that bus ride back to Asunción, on a deserted two-lane country road through soybean and cassava fields, I gazed out the window as my thoughts gave way simply to sharing the sunset with a mother and her young daughter. We did not speak the same language. Each attempt to connect through verbal communication fell short. All we could do was smile at one another. It was enough. The colors blending together in the violet sky somehow held it all.

In "Rain and the Rhinoceros," Merton continues to de-commodify the sound of rain. "The rain I am in is not like the rain of cities. It fills the woods with an immense and confused sound. It covers the flat roof of the cabin and its porch with insistent and controlled rhythms. And I listen, because it reminds me again and again that the whole world runs by rhythms I have not yet learned to recognize, rhythms that are not those of the engineer."

The Double Door Inn reminded me that all my measuring, all my linearizing, all my commodifying were perhaps part of life but not central to it. Nick had to pay his bills, but there was no commodifying powerful music . . . or land, or story.

I think our spiritual task is to listen to rhythms we have "not yet learned to recognize," to be animated by depth and beauty, color and sound. "Nobody started it, nobody is going to stop it," Merton concludes his essay. "It will talk as long as it wants, this rain. As long as it talks I am going to listen."

7

Kenosis

FIFTEEN MINUTES BEFORE THE Monday Night Allstars were scheduled to begin their set—which meant it would be a half hour before they began—I sat at the bar drinking an IPA. The quiet space felt like the ground around the burning bush.

But I learned from Mike the Bartender, a sixty-three-year-old man with rectangular glasses and a thick, white mustache and goatee, that this sacred place had seen its share of profane moments in its raucous rock-and-roll past.

As Rick Blackwell, bassist for the Monday Night Allstars, plopped down on a nearby stool, Mike rambled about some wild patron in the seventies who performed sexual acts on the bar-top which involved putting something in something else (one of those somethings was a beer bottle). Mike relished telling crude stories and describing the annoyance they caused other customers.

I could easily see Mike in Seinfeld's New York City apartment with George and Elaine, ranting about all the stupid people he bartended for each day—all the stupid things they said and all the stupid things they did and all the stupid amounts of alcohol they drank. Yet I could tell there was a part of him who loved the stupid people because he loved the sitcom they all lived in. Mike had worked at the Double Door for thirty-eight of its forty-four years. That's a lot of stories, most of which will remain unprinted.

I ordered another IPA. Something about just two beers, nothing more, frees me not to take myself too seriously. I once read a book called *The Pint Man*, by former *Sports Illustrated* columnist Steve Rushin, featuring an insecure man who became more comfortable in his skin, confident in his demeanor, and concerned with the needs of others the more beers he had at the local pub. I am a pint man, I think.

Thanks to my two beers I felt free to introduce myself to Rick and tell him how much I loved the Allstars. We struck up a lengthy conversation.

Rick was a thin, sixty-two-year-old African American with a slender face, narrow eyes, and a grayish white mustache and goatee. He always sang a few songs during the Allstars' set. His baritone voice was deep, smooth, and soothing. Before I knew it, he was telling me about the history of the Allstars. Rick had been with the band from the beginning and had also been best friends with the legendary Charles Hairston.

"What was he like?" I asked, thinking about the week before when Nick cried envisioning Charles making his way through the crowd, singing without a microphone.

Rick chuckled and shook his head, as if to say that words could never fully capture Charles' vibrant personality. "I met Charles through Ziad," he said, referring to the saxophonist for the Allstars. "Ziad had a band, and they needed a place to rehearse, so I let them do it at my house. When I first met Charles I was kind of leery of him. I didn't know what to think of him. He was very energetic. Always dancing. Kind of a showboater. Unpredictable."

"Years passed," he went on. "I hadn't seen Charles. And we eventually formed this band, the Les Moore Jam Session," which eventually became the Monday Night Allstars. "I would sing background for Charles, but when I sang he wouldn't really sing background for me. One time when I was singing, I noticed that people in the crowd lit up and started smiling. I thought it was for me, but then I looked behind me, and there's Charles doing all these dance moves. That's when I realized: that's who Charles is, he can't help it," Rick laughed.

"I keep a picture of him on my dining room table," Rick said. "Every morning, every time I pass him, I speak to him. I say, 'Charles Hairston!' And he used to say" [Rick's voice fluctuated], "*Heyyyyyy, Rick!* When I pass the table, that's what I hear."

"Why do you keep the picture there?" I asked, a personal question I never would have ventured without two beers.

"I loved that guy," Rick paused. "I guess maybe I need to take it off the table," he said sheepishly.

I shrugged and said, "I think maybe you should keep it there."

"I miss him," he reflected. "He started this whole thing."

In the early 2000s, Rick received a call while touring: "Your boy Charles Hairston got beat up downtown the other night." Rick called a mutual friend to see if he knew anything about the altercation. His friend confirmed the bad news.

"On Sunday I got back into town," Rick said, "and then on Monday with the Allstars, Charles was there on the gig! He had all his teeth knocked out. Had a big swell on his mouth. Eyes were swollen up. This, excuse me," Rick shook his head in comical dismay, "this mother f***er was still doing his thing, walking around and singing in the audience. He was still in everybody's face looking the way he looked—and singing! Just singing his ass off. That's what inspired me about Charles. He just gave his all no matter what, no matter if there was two people in the audience or two thousand. And I loved him for it."

Rick coughed and wiped his eyes.

"I get a little choked up about it now because Charles, man, he put a piece of God in your heart—and you could feel it. Charles is with me when I come here. He's still with me every Monday night. That's all I think about when I'm driving over here: Charles Hairston. I always think about the way he was . . . and what he did to me . . . and how he died."

Rick paused, stumbling upon another memory.

"The last night I was with him, in hospice, he couldn't respond to me, but he had the radio on. And I swear to you: every song that came on that radio was a song he had covered. *Every. Song.* I was just sitting there, kneeling at the bed, just crying and crying, and all of a sudden I heard Charles go, *hmmmmm, hmmmmm,* trying to hum to the song. He couldn't say anything, but I think he recognized that I was there. I think about that all the time."

I later heard from Ziad that "the only thing that mattered to Charles was a song." Whether without teeth or on his deathbed, no one could stop the legendary Charles Hairston from participating in what felt most true to him. To dare voice the rising song within is to make a claim: that truth is what pours into us—welling up in our souls—and it is powerful enough to break through our ego's dam and overflow into the world.

Franciscan philosopher St. Bonaventure conjures the image of "fountain fullness," a divine fountain of love and goodness at the core of reality, flowing *into* Creation, leaving watermarks or "vestiges" of divine beauty all around. The source of this fountain, Bonaventure says, is the dynamic, diverse, and creative relationship between God, Word, and Spirit, a non-conventional description of the conventional concept of the Trinity (enshrined in church tradition as Father, Son, and Holy Ghost). This all might seem overly intellectual or esoteric, but a metaphysical ultimate reality such as this is also an invitation: to partner with this creative force to heal ourselves and our world. I like to think of this cosmic deluge of love and goodness within relationship as rising and falling, like sound. Perhaps thin spaces are the conduits for this force, allowing love and goodness to flow into life's most broken scenes, like a man with a bruised and broken face singing to a crowd or humming on his deathbed to his best friend.

The Greek word used in the New Testament for this divine self-emptying is *kenosis*. True love always creates and then unites itself with its creation. The song that rose from Charles' soul brought him closer to his true self, his bandmates, the audience, and perhaps helped bring those who heard his song closer to their true selves and one another. As Merton wrote, "Art enables us to find ourselves and lose ourselves at the same time."[8]

Political activist and public intellectual Cornel West talks about the idea of "soulful kenosis" in the black musical tradition: John Coltrane "blowing his horn as if his neck is going to snap"; Al Green performing until he can no longer walk; Prince suffering chronic hip pain from jumping off pianos every night; James Brown performing for four-and-a-half hours straight. "He gives everything—every fiber of his being," West says of Brown, "and at the end of every concert, what does he say? 'I'm an extension of you, you're an extension to me, I don't exist without you.'"[9]

As God freely loves and gives, we can pour into one another's lives. Like Rick said of Charles, "He put a piece of God in your heart—and you could *feel* it."

8

Whoever Has Ears

THE FIRST TRACK ON PM #1, the CD Nick gave me featuring powerful music that was mostly recorded at the Double Door Inn, featured a strange exchange: a journalist's interview with country artist and renowned redneck Unknown Hinson.

"I don't play no rock," Unknown Hinson told the interviewer. "Naw, rock is straight out of hell. Country and western is my mission in life, baby. I know youngins likes that mess—yeah, yeah, but I wrote hundreds of songs with a fun, catchy beat that youngins like. It don't take no talent to play rock. Hell, any idiot can make that racket."

Baffled, the interviewer asked, "Now you say you don't like rock, and you don't like today's country, so what do you like?"

"What do I like?" he repeated. "Well you look pretty damn good yourself, little gal . . . I like, I don't know, a sunset in the evening, a pretty sunset. I like to hear the seal of a fresh fifth of liquor bein' popped. I like Cuban Heel Italian boots . . . I like the sound of a carnival—carnival's a pretty sound. I like the sound of doors slammin' and the tumblin' of locks."

I wonder what our lives would be like if we stopped and listened to the sounds of the day—to the clanking silverware, cicada choirs, the hum of tires on pavement, a dying street light buzzing, a kettle whistling?

"What do you like?" What if our answer was to walk slowly like we had nowhere to go, like the meeting could wait, like the to-do list was not in charge, like grocery-store monotony was our beach? What if our answer was just to listen? Would we hear the song that God sings?

When I try too hard to make sense of the world, I get stuck in my head—tangled up in ideas, theories, theologies. They have their place, but they easily can lead to obsessing over being right instead of in relationship.

What if we liked just to listen? What would America look like if we listened to those who were different from us, whose lives made sounds that were alien to us until we learned to recognize them?

"Whoever has ears, let them hear," Jesus once said to his disciples. I don't think he was talking about the literal sense of hearing; I think he was addressing paying attention to the interior life—to what gets pulled up from our own inner well, from the inner well of those we encounter in the sounds of the day.

Going to the Double Door Inn tuned my ears. In a thin place, I learned that the whole world is full of powerful music. Listening for it is nothing short of a spiritual discipline.

One Monday evening at the Double Door, I found myself observing four patrons who were there almost every week. There was the man with the perpetual smile and bouncing head whom Dave had pointed out to me as a symbol of freedom years before . . . a frizzy-haired, hippie-ish middle-aged woman who took up space to the right of the stage, gliding and spinning in her own little world . . . a petite, grandfatherly black man in a tweed flat cap who sometimes rose from his stool at the bar and twirled women around in ballroom fashion . . . and a skinny, pale, pony-tailed man in the corner, near the gliding hippie, who bounced up and down on his feet to the beat, rubbing his hands excitedly during guitar solos as if trying to stay warm.

For whatever reason, on this night I found myself mostly observing the pony-tailed bouncing man in the corner during the Allstars' set. Like the man with the bouncing head, I had never seen someone dance quite like the bouncing man, either. During each song, he was closing his eyes—and, well, bouncing—as he excitingly rubbed his hands together to the rhythm, sometimes raising those burning palms up to his mouth like a prayer. He was smiling too, often looking up at Joe Lindsay, the electric guitarist, in adoration.

After the first set, loosened by two IPAs, I approached him. "I see you here all the time," I said to him, extending my hand. He shook mine weakly, cautiously.

He told me his name and very little else. His speech was soft and slow, and his eyes were somewhat empty, uninterested, glazed. He seemed stoned. He was marked by such a joy while listening to music that I did not expect him to be so distant.

Trying to make conversation, I told him how much I loved the Double Door Inn.

"There are no words that can describe this place, man," he interrupted, shaking his head. "F***ing write that down." (I just did.)

I thought about his comment. Bouncing Man had just invited me into the heart of mysticism, whether he wanted to keep talking to me or not. I kept talking, because that's the thing about the pint man—with no one to impress, unafraid of looking like a fool, he can feel as free as the stoned man to say whatever he wants.

"So if something is unexplainable," I said, "is it worth even trying to explain it? This is what we as humans have been trying to do for so long, man: we've been trying to find words, whether to describe the divine or energy or the universe or whatever metaphor you want to use to describe the depth to life, to describe God. We keep trying to talk about it because we need to, not because we believe it's possible to adequately explain it. The Double Door Inn helps us both experience that great mystery."

Bouncing Man laughed, tilted his head and looked at me. "You know, you're all right, man."

I've always been more "all right" as a pint man than I am as a man.

We stood there for a little, not saying anything.

Then he turned to me and said, "Do you listen closely?"

Pint Man had won him over. Now *Bouncing Man* was making conversation.

"I'd like to listen more closely," I said. "I'd like to listen to the music like you listen to the music."

"Do you hear the echoes?" he asked again. "Or do you just play around on your f***ing phone?"

I laughed awkwardly. It was a fair critique of my generation.

"Do you ever bounce around in the songs?" he asked again. "Each song is like a roller-coaster for me."

I got the feeling Bouncing Man rode each song for its own unique thrill, and it didn't matter whether he had been to the theme park a hundred times.

"There's so much data in our subconscious," he continued. "I don't even have a television in my house. All I have is records. I just recently got back on Facebook, but I got rid of that for a while, too."

"It seems like you're a very present person," I said. "I'm trying to become a more present person."

"You have to listen closely," he said.

"Yeah," I said. "I need to listen closely."

"What the Double Door is, for me, is practice," he continued. "Practice for the present."

Then he reiterated, "It's about listening closely."

"Yeah, I need to listen closely," I confirmed.

When I was in high school, I went to punk-rock concerts. That was my first experience with crowd-surfing and moshing, which my friends and I thoroughly enjoyed in the invincibility of our youth.

It was never a question whether we were going to pick up some bruises. I can still remember that feeling of returning to earth once a band transitioned from an angry ballad of victimization to one of their slow groaning psalms of teenage heartbreak, bringing the moshing and surfing and jumping and screaming to a halt. I'd be dry-mouthed and light-headed as my ear drums pounded and my worn muscles screamed for rest. Being absorbed in the ocean of the moment did not come without a cost, yet it was worth every ache. The next day we would attempt to relive the concert by resorting to cheap descriptors like "amazing" or "phenomenal" or "wild."

"Wow," we'd say, "so amazing, so phenomenal, so wild, wow."

The experience had left a unique imprint on our minds, our hearts.

These days at concerts, people have their phones raised high above their heads, trying to capture an image or video rather than allowing the intimacy of the experience to create its own unique imprint on them.

To listen closely is to let sound rise up in our consciousness, in our *senses*. "God's presence is always hyper-presence," writes Peter Rollins. "This is analogous to the idea of a ship sunken in the depths of the ocean: while the ship contains the water and the water contains the ship, the ship only contains a fraction of the water while the water contains the whole of the ship. Our saturation by God does not merely fill us but also testifies to an ocean we cannot contain. Thus desire for God is born in God."[10] Author Esther de Waal puts it this way, "To listen closely, with every fibre of our being, at every moment of the day, is one of the most difficult things in the world, and yet it is essential if we mean to find the God whom we are seeking."[11]

To listen closely is to go where we have never gone before. To listen closely is to respond to what we've heard, even if that means picking up a couple bruises. We are not trying to capture anything. The ocean of the moment contains us, absorbs us. We venture into the song and see where it takes us.

9

All Is Music in a Music Room

ONE SUMMER AFTERNOON I was down in Dilworth, just south of uptown, when I caught sight of Ziad the saxophonist, informal ring-leader for the Monday Night Allstars, at a coffeeshop. I recognized him immediately because of his hat and glasses (did he ever take them off?). Ziad recognized me as the weirdo who kept showing up *alone* at the Double Door Inn a couple times a week. We shook hands and sat down next to a window, the summer heat bleeding through the open door. (In the South, it's impossible to make it past nine in the morning without sticky legs.)

Though Ziad Rabie did not look a day over forty, he was almost sixty the final year of the Double Door Inn, having gotten his philosophy degree in his twenties at Wake Forest University. Nick had raved to me about Ziad, which made me think he was probably more connected to the Double Door than any other musician. Every Monday with the Allstars and every Tuesday with Bill Hanna's jazz band, Ziad was there, playing his sax. He was as well-known nationally as he was locally, having recorded with legends like James Brown and Gospel Music Hall of Fame recording artist John P. Kee. He had also shared the stage with (or opened for) some of the most renowned contributors in jazz and soul music—people like Herbie Hancock, Gladys Knight, Grover Washington Jr., Ramsey Lewis, and Aretha Franklin.

Ziad was one cool cat.

"I've seen you a lot lately around the Double Door," Ziad said curiously, sipping his coffee.

I tried to tell Ziad what the Double Door meant to me, hardly coherent, I'm sure, in my caffeine buzz. "For the last five years, the Double Door has had a way of re-centering me. It's helped me to see reality more clearly." And then I went on about true realities and false realities, true selves and false selves, which came from the heart, but probably sounded like philosophical gobbledygook.

What I was trying to say to Ziad was that because the Double Door Inn had a legacy of being unashamedly itself in a world that felt largely fake—filled with people, businesses, and systems operating out of shallow, self-focused motives—it continually inspired me to become more fully myself, to partner with the cosmic force of love.

"You're saying some heavy stuff," Ziad eventually commented in his strong, deep voice. "The Double Door represents a forty-three-year tradition of that freedom you're talking about—that genuine authenticity, and there is something to be said for that. The Double Door Inn is a music room. People come there for one thing: music. Not many places in Charlotte like that."

"How about you?" I said. "When did you start going to the Double Door?"

Ziad grinned, his eyes shifting to the ceiling, or perhaps the sky.

"The first time I ever went there, I was a senior in high school," he reflected. "This was sometime in the mid seventies, and I remember going to the Double Door to see this group called Moose Magic—George Shaw and John Wilhelm—and two weeks after I saw them, they were tragically killed in a car accident. Two of the brightest stars in this area, man. There's no telling what their futures would've held. Their creativity and talent were limitless, and there was so much forward motion. Anyway, they were on stage playing, and they were going from a Chick Corea song to a Beatles song like 'I Want To Hold Your Hand,' and I'm thinking 'This is the coolest thing I've ever seen.'"

"And at the end of the last set, this famous bluegrass fiddle player named Vassar Clements—he had heard that they were there and was looking for a place to sit in or something—went up to the stage, this stocky guy with red-and-white plaid pants and a navy blue polyester mock turtleneck, and they all start playing 'Spain' by Chick Corea. It was just so eye-opening to me to think that this bluegrass guy knew Chick Corea. It opens up everything. Think about that. You know what I'm saying? It's like, it's all music, you know?"

Ziad had walked through the philosophical door I opened.

I asked him why it was so transformative for him to see Moose Magic playing songs from all across the musical spectrum and a hillbilly fiddler playing a Chick Corea song. As a young saxophonist pursuing the complexities of jazz, Ziad sometimes trapped himself in the genre or became ultra-critical of his progress. At the Double Door, categories fell away. Musicians who may have been labeled one way—connected to a particular genre by fans or by their record label—stepped into the Double Door and freely ruptured expectations.

"The Double Door was subconsciously and consciously a way for me to realize that the authenticity and genre of the music were more important than how many notes you could play or how many chords or scales you knew," Ziad said. "There was a bigger purpose . . . I could go anywhere if I had an open mind."

Nothing crosses categories we construct quite like music. Mike the Bartender's partner behind the bar, Reid, would later tell me the Double Door Inn was the most diverse place in Charlotte. He was probably right. There was a dizzying mix of race, age, gender, and thought in that place. In a polarized age where identity is crucial to conversation—sometimes for good reason (say, to discuss economic disparity) but often times used to demonize "the other" in our rampant caricaturing—music and art can make identity-obsessed people deeply uncomfortable. Music cuts through divisions, settling in common into the souls of people who on paper could not be more different.

Before we left the coffeeshop, Ziad said to me, "Music has the power and capacity to enlighten people because it puts them in touch with their emotions and who they are. It's a refuge from everything that makes them have to be who they are not. Look at some of the great musical stars, Aretha Franklin, for example—these are people who are always motivated by spirit. The Double Door was a house for music that brought the spirit into those four walls and under that roof—and that's where the meaning is. I guess what I'm saying is that music pulls me deeper into being."

10

A New Kind of Listening

As BILL HANNA'S TUESDAY night jazz band began to play, Mike the Bartender cracked open another IPA and slid it over to me. It had been a year since I attended Tuesday night jazz at the Double Door Inn, the last time on a date. She was a musician, and I suppose I wanted her to think I had sophisticated hearing. That night she began to realize how very sophisticated I was.

Then we began seriously dating, and she saw me scream obscenities during an Indianapolis Colts game . . . and flip off the television during an Indiana University basketball game . . . and write memoir and play golf—that beautiful, brutal sport—and root for the Chicago Cubs to solidify my masochism. What is dating but the fading of perceived sophistication?

Anyway, I had always liked jazz, but I rarely craved it. I thought I needed to be in a particular mood for jazz. It was kind of like meditation: usually freeing, eventually, yet hardly the emotional high of pulsing rock. Most in my generation attend concerts because we are, in some way, familiar with the songs a band plays. We might like it when the band does something unexpected, say, take an extended jam at the end of a song or blend a couple of songs together, but our expectations are based on an underlying familiarity.

Jazz, on the other hand, is pure improvisation. It is vast, complex, and meanders freely without agenda. Not even the jazz band knows where the river is flowing, other than toward paradox, between the banks of chaos and order. It requires a different, attentive kind of listening. As Sebastian (played by Ryan Gosling) excitedly says in *La La Land*, "It's conflict and it's compromise, it's new every time."

Jazz can be uncomfortable because it dares me to hoist my familiar anchors and let myself be guided into the open sea. In the outstretched nothingness of the ocean, where east becomes west and north becomes south, the middle and end of my journey remain unknown. It's just me and the water. This sailing across a vast landscape demands full presence. I tend to remain in my mind, but with jazz I've learned it's my *senses,* rather than my thoughts or emotions, that are a portal into the thin space that has found me.

James Baldwin wrote beautifully about the sensual dimension of blues and jazz—how most Americans struggle to embrace these genres because they are trapped in a listening binary where "happy songs are happy and sad songs are sad," where white Americans in particular "are terrified of sensuality, and do not any longer understand it."[12] On sensuality, Baldwin wrote, "To be sensual, I think, is to respect and rejoice in the force of life, of life itself, and to be present in all that one does, from the effort of loving to the breaking of bread."

Bill Hanna, Charlotte's "Godfather of Jazz," conducted the stage that evening, as the music meandered along, unfolding wherever it felt like going. The Godfather, a ball of a man with a furry, pale face and big glasses, looked like he wasn't a day over sixty though he was well past eighty. He mostly played keyboard but sometimes hopped on trombone. In between songs, he often rambled incomprehensibly, leaving the audience bewildered and mirroring the lack of finality in jazz, before resuming playing music again.

Throughout the jam session, he'd call people from the audience to the stage, many times his former students, to play along with him. Ziad accompanied the Godfather throughout the entire set; without Bill, there was no Ziad. The Godfather had taught Ziad the twelve-bar blues. Throughout the night I saw musicians "go out on their own," yet their wandering was only as good as their listening, their hands and fingers only as good as their ears. Anyone at anytime could "be themselves" as long as they remained humbly held together by the whole. The drummer was the time-keeper who held the song together, simultaneously providing a benediction to wander off and an invitation to come home.

It took an hour until I allowed myself to surrender that evening. In Ziad's words, I let jazz "pull me deeper into being"—rupturing my comfort, shuffling my labeling. For me, opening my senses felt like leaving my mind behind: listening to the sounds without intellectualizing what they might mean, touching my feet on the worn, dirty floors and grounding them in the moment, feeling the brimming energy as a spirit-led musician wandered from the fold and improvised, tasting each ounce of my IPA.

St. Bonaventure wrote that our senses are conduits to divine intimacy—pathways to experiencing our own union with God. Robust spirituality is an embodied experience—integrating the entirety of the human person, not just engaging our mind. One of my dear friends, a Franciscan friar named Fr. Dan Riley, says that Christians have often narrowed "reading the Word" to pertain only to scripture, which limits reading to mostly a mental exercise.[13] Yet humans throughout history were reading the eternal Word—*logos*—long before the invention of the printing press. Our ancestors read the Created Order around them: in the shifting wind, in the smell of rain, in the migration of animals, in the joy or fear on the human face, in the multidimensional meaning contained in ikons, mosaics, and oral stories. Until recently, humans have always read with their senses.

In the House of Rising Sounds

Jazz, I've come to learn, is like the rain Merton wrote about. Rhythms rise yet remain uncontrolled. Patterns shift and evolve, always inviting listeners into the newness of the moment. It is "gratuitous and meaningless." There is no formula for it.

After the jazz session, I approached the stage to say hello to Ziad. Like a bouncer checking his VIP list into an exclusive nightclub, Ziad introduced me to Bill and suggested that we spend some time together. Bill rambled on about something I did not understand. I nodded continuously, which I tend to do when I don't understand someone, unsure what I'm agreeing to.

He told me to swing by his classroom on Wednesday. That, I understood.

1 1

It's Your Own Solo

THE NEXT DAY, I parked at the Double Door Inn and walked across the street onto the Central Piedmont campus. I entered a tall brick-and-cast-stone building, glowing burnt orange in the afternoon sun, asked a faculty member where I might find Bill Hanna, and was guided up a flight of stairs. Pushing open the door, I peered down the steps of a high-ceilinged classroom with stadium seating. Perched below me at his grand piano was the Godfather. He looked up through his buggy, wire-framed glasses. He looked back down and continued playing piano, perhaps his version of hello.

I thought of the students who had walked through those same doors at the dawn of a semester to have their lives changed by the man at the bottom of the stairs. I thought of Ziad—what he'd learned from the Godfather sent him out to share his gifts but also brought him back every Tuesday to play alongside his mentor. The point of going on the inward journey to discover deep-seated treasures is to eventually toss those treasures into a collective chest that benefits the community—to share what we've discovered, to collaborate, to give back to the world.

For twenty years the Godfather had taught at Central Piedmont. For thirty years before that, he'd taught band and orchestra at Charlotte Mecklenburg Schools. He didn't seem to be slowing down. At eighty-three, he was the opposite of brittle and bare. He had short, white hair and a sturdy physique, his plain black shirt and sterling silver necklace suggesting he was about to speed off on a Harley. Someone told me the Godfather still flew his Cessna-150, sometimes just to take a friend a state or two away to get some barbecue for lunch.

I told the Godfather how much I loved the Double Door Inn. I told him that I was learning to love jazz. That was enough to get us going.

The Godfather shared that he started hosting jazz sessions around Charlotte in the sixties. He said Nick's establishment was one of the few places in Charlotte that allowed jazz to exist as it is. Whereas so many other venues in Charlotte had stipulations for the Godfather and his jazz band, like the steakhouse he told me about that forced them to wear suits and ties and to refrain from tenor saxophone and "sappy music"—those "slow moving, beautiful ballads"—the Double Door did not try to manufacture the experience or "push the river," as Richard Rohr writes. It welcomed the messiness and mystery that is jazz. And if there was one person who had always longed to improvise and float freely through the musical stratosphere, it was the Godfather, which made jazz a perfect fit for him.

"A plight of jazz musicians all along is that they had trouble playing what they wanted to play," the Godfather told me from his piano stool. "When I first got off the road and started playing gigs down in the southeast, they wouldn't hire me because I had a black drummer. Back in those days, you couldn't have a mixed crew. And then there were all the criticisms when we did play: 'You're playing too loud! You're playing too fast! Can't you play something slow? We're not happy with this music!' But that's what's beautiful about the Double Door: nobody says that there. We play what we want to play."

The Godfather burst into a piano solo then paused, "Jazz is improvisation, plain and simple. You make the notes that either sound good or sound bad. That's another beautiful thing about jazz, being able to create a melody, spur of the moment, that has highs and lows, fast and slow, and it's yours—it's your own solo."

It's your own solo, I repeated in my head.

The fourteenth-century Scottish philosopher John Duns Scotus had a word for the particularity of creation: *haecceitas*, or "thisness." In other words, each particular aspect of creation sings its own song, plays its own solo. It is all for us to hear. In thinness there is *thisness*.

That day that I'd visited Iguazu Falls, every individual aspect of creation seemed to play its own solo to me. It was not only the symphony of the whole crashing around me through hundreds of waterfalls. It was the serenity of the outstretched rainbow; the gentle butterfly perching itself on my friend Jamie's finger; Coach Briscoe's beaming smile; the mist kissing my cheek before fading into the gulley; the scavenging coatis, South America's version of a rodent, digging through trashcans; the pattering footsteps of pilgrims on the path. It was jazz.

So overwhelming were the sights and sounds at the Falls, especially for a Hoosier who grew up surrounded by cornfields and basketball courts, that my awareness magnified each solo around me. The truth is that all was already alive, which is to say it was a "vestige," as St. Bonaventure suggests—a divine remnant, a thumbprint, a portal—but now each diverse expression of creation seemed to show itself to me, beautiful and vulnerable.

I like to think that Creation is a symphony of sound, each unique created being playing its own solo. We, as collaborators (not conductors) in the orchestra, are invited to contemplate the creative expression of the Word as it is revealed to us: in the particularity of smiles, songs, stories, creatures, sacred spaces, and everyday places.

Our desire for uniformity suggests that we are afraid of this diversity, this freedom among one another. We want the collective song we sing to be systematic, controlled; not meander into the unknown as jazz does and will always do. Our nation's founders, with all their flaws, had it right when their core efforts led them to the motto, *e pluribus unum*: out of many, one. They may as well have been describing jazz more than one hundred years before it was birthed by African-American musicians in New Orleans. Jazz is who we are.

We know, deep down, that we are each diverse expressions of this strange democratic experiment, that each of us has something unique to offer to the song we play, and that it's only because of this diversity and particularity that we are one. Pope Francis encourages us to listen with ears of our hearts, a deep form of listening that integrates attentiveness to the Other: "Listening," he writes, "always requires the virtue of patience, together with the ability to allow oneself to be surprised by the truth, even if only a fragment of truth, in the person we are listening to. Only amazement enables knowledge."[14]

Out of many, one. Why do we keep letting politicians and legacy media divide us by our differences for their own financial gain? How has our Information Age often made us more certain rather than more humble and curious? Let the progressives wander from the fold and rupture labels as they discover new avenues of song. Let the conservatives *conserve* patterns within the song that hold the whole together. Let it all belong. Let *haecceitas* thrive. Let jazz reign.

12

Inner Jazz Artist

SEATED ON HIS PIANO stool, the Godfather told me he was always longing to improvise. When he began taking piano lessons in elementary school, his instructor would get upset because he would "hear other things between the notes" and play them. He liked piano but would eventually walk away from the ivory keys in grade school out of shame—when boys in his class began calling him a "sissy" because of his affinity for music. A natural burden of art, I guess—femininity—though no longer a burden to me, but rather a pathway, I'm convinced, to the True Self. As Thomas Merton wrote, "The feminine principle in the world is the inexhaustible source of creative realizations of the Father's glory . . . But she remains unseen, glimpsed only by a few. Sometimes there are none who know her at all."[15]

It was through the gateway of shame the Godfather became re-engaged with the piano and his fascination with jazz, albeit two decades later, when, like any sissy, he joined the army. One evening at Fort Jackson in Columbia, South Carolina, the Godfather witnessed a jazz session unfold in his barrack. Confidently thinking he could dabble because of his many years playing the trombone in the marching band, he asked the leader if he could join. Yes.

"I went up there to perform and, man, I stepped all over myself," the Godfather admitted. "I heard the music, had all these ideas in my head, but I could not find them on the trombone. Afterwards, the leader said to me, 'If you wanna play this kind of music, boy, you're gonna to have to learn how to practice.' That always stuck with me. I said to myself, 'That's what I want to do—I want to learn how to be an improvisor.' I wanted to play jazz. I wanted to belong to that small, little, esoteric group. Rock and Roll is a big group. Jazz is a small group. I like belonging to the small group. I like to do things my own way. I don't want to follow the crowd."

Before he knew it, the Godfather found himself serving in the fourth infantry division in Frankfurt, Germany. He and his platoon sat in on downtown jazz clubs to watch the German, Italian, and French musicians play together. This only piqued the Godfather's interest in what would become his craft and life's work.

Any apprentice needs a master, and the Godfather found his across the hall in a pianist named Tom. The master encouraged his apprentice to listen to everything he could. Once a month the Godfather would spend his paycheck at a record store in downtown Frankfurt. Like any form of progression or enlightenment, the initial portal to the Godfather's musical transformation was through a simple yet profound posture: active, attentive listening.

The Godfather finished his service, returned to the States, completed his business degree at Davidson College, then enrolled in Indiana University, a "dang good music school," to pursue his master's in music and trombone. Yet this time there would be no jazz, as his trombone instructor, another "Tom" figure, was classically trained and made sure that his students were, too.

"One night I was practicing in the university music room," the Godfather said, starting to play his piano again, "you know, playing a little dahhhhh-dahhhhh-dahhhhh, and then I'd go dahh-hhhh-boo-do-didladoo-doo-dahhhhh-doodla-do-doodla-do-dah-hhhh. Putting a little *feel* in it, ya know! Well, Tom was walking by outside, stuck his head through the window, and said, 'No jazz, Bill!'"

"The reason he didn't like jazz is because he couldn't play it. And he was jealous of all his students who could. He could pick off a double-high f-bend on the trombone—rock solid—but take the page away, and he was lost."

One benefit of this suppression of jazz is that the Godfather got bored. Strict formulas ripped mystery right out of music, and the Godfather began looking for a new challenge. He began playing piano once more. If he was prohibited from playing jazz on his trombone, then he'd learn a new instrument, for the future purpose of jazz.

"I guess I should thank Tom, because that's why I'm playing piano today," the Godfather laughed.

It often happens that some innate longing in our lives seems too obscure, too "out there," too different to be within easy reach. Pursuing it requires courage in the face of an unknown outcome. Our sacrifice and energy might not be acceptable by conventional standards or "successful" through a performative mindset. Yet the longings closest to our hearts are paradoxically liberating and excruciating—what often finds expression in jazz.

I think that this ambiguity is not only a fundamental part of jazz but also core to our own journeys. As Donald Miller famously began in his bestselling book *Blue Like Jazz*, "I never liked jazz music because jazz music doesn't resolve."[16] Though my credibility begins and ends with how music makes me feel, my understanding is that jazz is a genre that incorporates dissonance—the discordant blending of notes—unlike any other. I wonder if what feels discordant or unharmonious on our creative journeys might in fact be the building blocks for dissonance and an unexpected kind of beauty and relief?

The Godfather stuck it through at IU and got his esteemed degree. A series of unlikely events led to an opportunity to fill in for a trombone player in legendary jazz musician Stan Kenton's jazz big band. When the trombone player returned, Stan, impressed by Bill's abilities, recommended the Godfather to Woody Herman, another famous jazz musician. All it took was Stan's trusted word for Woody to welcome the Godfather into the band.

In Woody's band, everything within the Godfather seemed to click into place, as he performed several solos each night. Finally, he was playing a style of music he had always dreamed of. No more rules and stipulations. No more professors breathing down his neck. It was jazz at its finest and the Godfather at his finest, an experience that would eventually inspire over five decades of teaching and cultivating jazz in Charlotte, North Carolina.

Creativity, in my experience, is having the courage to uncover (an inward process) and unleash (an outward process) the deepest, most authentic parts of yourself. Call it your "Inner Jazz Artist." You can tell if it's authentic or not by whether it's grounded in love and service. Thin spaces send us on a journey of cultivating this Inner Jazz Artist so music might flow through us more easily, as we learn to become conduits.

The Double Door Inn helped cultivate the Godfather's Inner Jazz Artist, and because the Godfather had a space where he could be who he is, the Godfather could then cultivate the Inner Jazz Artist in others, for he was more in touch with himself, more alive, thanks to welcoming places. He was forming in his students what those places had formed in him.

We all need spaces in our world where our Inner Jazz Artist can thrive—where judgment and fear to take a backseat to playing whatever we want to play. The key word is "play."

13

Abbeys of Chaos

IT WOULD BE EASY to romanticize thin spaces, but they are also disorienting. They are not temporary escapes of boosted emotional highs. They are not altar calls that attempt to bandage gaping wounds with promises of wholeness. They disrupt life as usual, permanently.

Thin places humble us by reminding us that we don't know what we don't know, or perhaps that we no longer need to know anything. The first time Dave took me to the Double Door, the freedom I experienced also forced me to see all the ways in which I was not free. The intimate connectedness I experienced on many nights did not come without vulnerability—an almost terrifying confrontation with my own smallness, with my own nothingness in the presence of depth and beauty, what I call *depeauty*.

Thin spaces don't massage our egos; they shatter them. At the Double Door, I felt like I lost control, spiraling around and around toward the core—quite the dizzying ride—as my senses invited my mind to let go. Many intellectual pursuits have helped to expand my curiosity and empathy. But many times I have needed my senses to guide me out of my head back to an embodied spiritual experience.

In the House of Rising Sounds

When I first heard the term "contemplative," I envisioned a monk-like figure sitting around and thinking all day. I thought to myself, *I can be a contemplative—all I do is contemplate, maybe I was born to be a monk.* That sentiment didn't land me many second dates. Maybe thinking all the time is just anxiety masked with intellectualism. Contemplation, I've learned, is pretty much the opposite of what I thought it was. As Zen Master Winnie the Pooh once said, "Doing nothing often leads to the very best of something."

To be a modern contemplative, I think, is to construct abbeys in our daily lives—everyday places that might become thin spaces—which help us not to escape, but rather to plunge deeper into reality through the gifts of silence, solitude, and stillness (doing nothing), detached from whatever it is we might be using to convince ourselves of our worth. I think one way to know whether we're gaining a false sense of worth from something—whether we're commodifying something—is if it has become an unhealthy or desperate escape. I would agree with the Buddhists that my attachments are usually the root of my suffering.

Abbeys are not euphoric escapes. Maybe they help us find peace and a deeper sense of self—a deeper sense of union with God—but that almost always entails letting go. Abbeys strip us of our attachments, leaving us naked in the moonlight, exposed, yet in this vulnerability we might encounter the truth we've been searching for all along.

All of this is why true mysticism shouldn't be misunderstood as woo-woo oneness. On his "Everything is Spiritual" tour, Rob Bell explained that for 13.7 billion years the universe has been expanding in unity, depth, and complexity.[17] This is true on a molecular and atomic level but also, as I can see it, on a spiritual level. You might know that you've brushed up against a truth in the universe—that you're in a thin place—when you experience a sense of connectedness (unity), yet this awareness will likely sling you down the spiral (depth) into chaos (complexity).

My first time on silent retreat at the Abbey of Gethsemani, I remember being struck by the large motto visible to anyone walking up the brick pathway toward the steps of the abbey doors, hanging above the gate of the adjacent garden: "GOD ALONE." These two words perfectly describe the contemplative life that monks find at the abbey, the essence of thin spaces. As philosopher Peter Rollins has pointed out, you can't spell "all one" without the letters "a-l-o-n-e."[18]

The year the Double Door Inn was set to close, I took a brief sabbatical from my abbey of choice and went with my friends to Chicago, that city that has beckoned to me ever since I was a little boy at my first Cubs game at Wrigley Field. In high school my peers and I roamed those streets endlessly during a journalism conference. In college I'd take the train from the South Bend station with thirty dollars in my pocket—a week's pay at the campus newspaper—to ice-skate at Millennium Park and split a deep-dish pizza at Giordano's. Chicago never failed to dazzle me with the speckled glow of its ambition, quenching within me some deep need for adventure, but also rooted in Midwestern charm, reminding me of my Indiana home.

Now, Nathan and I lagged behind as we walked down Michigan Avenue, the girls in front of us dressed in short skirts and boots, leading us toward some upscale nightclub with city views that cost twenty dollars just to board the elevator. Their glee rose up into the heavy breeze that blew in from the lake and now tunneled down those lively streets. Doing what two grown men sometimes do when prowling such a splendid city—a few drinks in, gearing up for a night of dancing—we pulled out our phones to catch a shitload of Pokemon. I wasn't a fan of nightclubs, but I could have wandered the town with Nathan all evening, catching invisible animals.

At the nightclub, I found myself drifting from the group, acting like I was going to get another drink from the bar—having sipped on my first for a good ninety minutes, now warm and tasting increasingly piss-like—but not wanting to pay twenty dollars for a bourbon. I sat for a moment on a black couch next to one of those extravagant floor-to-ceiling windows, overlooking that city I loved.

But this time I was not looking down into the streets lined with taxi-cabs, nor out on the river sprinkled with the lights of boats peacefully sauntering by. I looked at all the strangers around me. The beats throbbed. The lights flashed. The girls were taking selfies, turning to the side, cocking their heads, arching their backs, then immediately crowding around the phone to evaluate the picture, either retaking it to compensate for their "mistakes" or posting it right away on social media for their fantasized version of themselves to be affirmed.

I looked out at inebriated men and saw lustful eyes, perfectly-gelled hair, casual awareness of their surroundings. Were they inhabiting their bodies, I wondered? Or were they hungry to see their own fantasized version of themselves in a stranger's eyes, in their next sexual conquest?

That night it seemed to me that all these people were chasing escapes when what they needed were abbeys. I remembered how philosopher Peter Rollins commented that if the thumping beats of a nightclub came to a screeching halt and all the lights flashed on, absolving our own shadows, might we all, for a second, come into contact with our own emptiness?[19]

Rollins juxtaposes nightclubs with an Irish pub, where a sad singer-songwriter might croon an anguished tale of love lost, which might lead one listener to confide in another about their own fractures of the heart. Contrary to the nightclub, the music and drinks at an Irish pub are less escape mechanisms than tools for more fully engaging the complexity and traumas of life.

Careful listening—to the next song, to our friend, to a stranger—guides us into that vulnerable space. When the musician has played the last song or we've had our last pint, we emerge from the pub with a renewed sense of direction, having made contact with a unitive, deep, complex truth. We take a line from a song or a revelation from our conversation into our lives. The night at the pub was wonderful, sure. Maybe the musician was talented or the new beer on tap was tasty, but then again, maybe we've been to the pub twice a week for five years straight, or heard the same sad song by the same musician a hundred times, or were just drinking two-for-one Michelob Ultras. Maybe the atmosphere of the pub opened up our senses and hearts and minds, but it was our own vulnerability—our own willingness to be cracked open—that made the pub a thin space.

I could not help but think about the Double Door Inn that evening in its very antithesis, the Chicago nightclub. The outside of the Double Door's sanctuary was far from flashy or attractive to the eye, unconcerned with appearances because the inside was bursting with life. The message from the altar did not fuel people's escapes as they chased the myths of attention and affection; it invited them into unity, depth, and complexity—the catalyst for all to experience something transcending. And bourbons, it must be said, were only four or five dollars.

But then I looked over at all my friends, dancing in the corner, and thought about all the Pokemon that Nathan and I we were going to catch that evening. I thought about how our stories had mysteriously intersected with one another in Charlotte and were now being woven together through new experiences in this absurdly flashy nightclub. He had a way of accepting me as I was in our friendship, genuinely curious to learn about where I was coming from without judgment even if he disagreed. What mattered was our invested hearts, not our differing opinions. I smiled and remembered that, despite my disgust for that fake place, I had been gifted with the present moment with my beautiful friends in that splendid town. I returned to the group with a bourbon and disappeared into the sounds.

14

Players Gonna Play

I WALKED INTO THE Double Door Inn one evening and saw Shana Blake, lead singer for the Monday Night Allstars, sitting at the bar sipping a Pabst Blue Ribbon, always her drink of choice on stage. For years I had been moved by her performances, and not just by her voice, which was damned near flawless, but also by her spirit—the way she glowed from the stage, always dancing, always smiling . . . and off the stage, too, as she often left her microphone in the middle of a song to hug the regular patrons or dance with those in the crowd—the ones who, as she always said, were willing to "leave it all out on the dance floor."

I introduced myself and got a "Great to meet ya darlin'" hug with a genuine smile. Shana had that southern-woman way of calling everyone by "sweetie," "darlin," "honey," or "love," one of the many reasons I fell for the Carolinas. Where else in the country could you stuff your face with chicken and waffles or biscuits and gravy and walk out of the diner with an ego boost, thinking to yourself, *Did you hear the way that waitress called me sweetie?*

Shana and I began talking about the Double Door Inn, and she eventually asked me if I wanted to go outside and sit on the back deck.

"Sure," I said.

The cool air kissed our cheeks. Shana took a cigarette from her jacket pocket.

"Do you mind?" she asked politely.

"Of course not," I said. I didn't mind cigarette smoke, especially if it was coming from the mighty lungs of Shana Blake.

Shana's head of thick, strawberry-blonde curly hair framed her pretty freckled face and beer-bottle-brown eyes. Tonight she seemed shy and soft-spoken, as if feeling out whether I could be entrusted with her story.

"I grew up with stage fright," she eventually admitted. This surprised me, considering her confidence behind the microphone.

"Years ago in my first band," she continued, "in between songs, I would try to look as busy as I possibly could so that I didn't have to speak into the microphone to the crowd. I also used to close my eyes when I sang so I couldn't see the crowd. It's been a long process to get back to myself, to just be myself on stage, to not think about it or try to perform."

There it was again: our deep need to get back to who we are in the deepest recesses of our being: beloved, enough, and unashamed. Reclaiming the parts of ourselves that got clouded as we journeyed through the world. Uncovering what resides within the evolving house. Loss stuns; rejection cripples; shame paralyzes. Somewhere along the way, maybe shame sent Shana Blake into hiding. Luckily for her, the Double Door Inn had invited her to come on out.

When Shana was a student at Central Piedmont Community College—the campus that was now swallowing our shack of music— she would drop by the Double Door some afternoons to grab a beer between classes. At that time, her visits had less to do with music than with cheap beer, vital fuel for college kids.

But she'd always had an affinity for music despite her nervousness and stage fright, so she pursued her passion in the shadows. In the late nineties, she collaborated on a project with the legendary Charles Hairston. "He kept telling me about this 'Monday Night Allstar' thing," Shana laughed. So one Monday evening, she went to see them, and like most first-time visitors she was seized by wonder and awe. She began attending every week. It became her version of church.

"I love music, and I love people," Shana said. "The band was dynamic but Charles just commanded the stage. He would spin. He would sweat. It was such a loving atmosphere. Ego was nowhere to be found."

Sometimes Charles would call her up to the stage to sing a duet, usually Stevie Wonder's "Tell Me Something Good."

"It'd be terrible, every time," Shana said self-deprecatingly. "It was the wrong key, but I would do it every time just to be up there singing with him."

Neither of them knew, but this scene was a picture of both the past and the future of the Allstars.

As Shana continued to evolve as a musician, the Double Door Inn remained her safe haven—a place for her to dance and sing and enjoy music in its purest form. Little did she know that this place where she learned to combat the world's lies and her own false self was preparing her to give as a performer what she had received as a consumer.

"After Charles passed away in 2009, I took a little break from this place," Shana said. "It was hard to be here after that."

The Allstars didn't want to split after Charles's death. But his passing left a massive void, impossible shoes to fill, not only for the band, but for those who loved Monday nights. They tried a number of different male singers. "Each had a different vibe and style and were great singers, but people just wanted Charles," Shana reflected.

Finally, the Allstars flipped the script—to go with a female voice instead of a male voice. And the first person who came to mind was Shana Blake.

In September 2012, Jim Brock, the Cherokee drummer, sent her a text saying, "Would you like to join us on Monday nights?," a text that Shana still had saved on her phone four years later. She agreed. Now the only person in the way of Shana Blake was Shana Blake.

"My first year singing with them, it was real difficult for me," Shana said. "They were the *Monday Night Allstars* and had done all this great stuff. And I was this nobody, hometown girl. So it took me a while to build my confidence, I think—to truly feel like I was a part of it. It was a big mental barrier."

She had arrived at the great crossroads of journeying back to herself.

"As far as the anxiety that goes along with stage fright, that was heightened when I joined the Allstars," she said. "But now what's heightened is that I feel a lot like Charles up there. I don't know if his spirit is there or if maybe it's because I've always loved him, but we share that simple love for people and for music. And the music we create helps us to love each other more and accept each other more."

"I try not to think about success—I try to get up there and be as 'me' as I possibly can. It's fun to just do your thing and not worry about missing a note—to just be yourself. Success may or may not come. Failure may or may not come. The goal is to sing as authentically as you can. This place taught me how to be comfortable being myself."

I had felt it before, too, that stage fright—that strange disconnect-edness—brought on by the imposter. When I began constructing my walls, I built them around the greatest gift God gave me—a heart so full, so eager, so willing; a heart that had always led the way, fueling risks and foolish leaps of faith; a heart that left me utterly exposed on doorsteps, singing for locked doors. So I buried my prized possession and retreated into my mind. Ideas and logic are easier to control than love and longing, dreams and desires.

"Someone once told me that the ears are the first thing to fully develop on a fetus," Shana told me in our back-deck conversation. "Well, first, it's your spinal column and then, nerve endings, but after that, it's your ears. By the time you are born, you've already started moving away from yourself. It takes you years and lots of questioning to get back to that spirit of innocence and acceptance, which is through hearing and choosing to listen."

If it was shame that locked my inner child in a cupboard under the stairs like Harry Potter, joy has been my key to release. We sure found it at Iguazu. Jamie was suddenly playing with butterflies. I was opening my mouth to taste the mist of waterfalls. Coach Briscoe couldn't stop smiling and laughing. I often find it at the Double Door, as I release my inner child to roam and play. Watching Shana perform, I join her freedom on the playground, having a good time with anyone who wants to do the same. We let go of inhibition and give magic a chance.

15

High Priestess of Sympathy

IT HAD BEEN A couple of weeks since I talked to Shana. We'd been texting back and forth about the Double Door Inn, music, and journeying back to oneself. I was struck she took our first conversation so seriously, allowing its contents to continue to stir her within.

Sitting at the bar one evening, I felt a gentle nudge on my shoulder. I turned around and felt my face light up.

"Hey there darlin,'" Shana beamed, opening her arms, then pulling up a barstool next to me. "I thought you might be here."

"Two PBRs," I called to Reid.

After some small talk, Shana told me she'd been thinking again about our conversation. "I want to show you something," she said, pulling out her phone.

She invited me to look over her shoulder. On the screen were three separate tabs. "Here's the first video," she said, clicking on a tab.

Five metronomes were lined up along a wooden paddle, ticking away unsynchronized. Then someone picked up the paddle and balanced it across two empty soda cans on their sides. Within seconds, the metronomes synchronized with one another. In music, this was called *sympathy*, Shana explained. The freedom the metronomes had atop the shifting tin cans allowed them to mysteriously synchronize—or sympathize—with one another, forming a unified clicking sound.

I remembered hearing someone call Shana the "High Priestess of Sympathy." It made sense now. Every Monday, her vocals, her dancing, her presence, her spirit, pulled the audience deeper into being. It invited the crowd to enter into synchronization, into sympathy.

"It gets crazier," she said, opening another tab.

This video explained a scientific study that explored the emergence of collective consciousness, revealing itself through the synchronization of people's heartbeats who were singing together in choir. Like those metronomes placed upon the tin cans, the study revealed that it didn't take long for people's heartbeats to synchronize. It quoted Björn Vickhoff, a scientist of neurophysiology: "When people sing together, their hearts start beating at the same pace . . . And every time people get together, for example at a football stadium, some type of collective consciousness is formed."[20]

I looked over at Shana and raised my glass. She smiled and clanked mine.

"Here's the last one," she said, clicking the final tab.

Patrons were slowly beginning to fill the Double Door and order drinks at the bar. Ziad was warming up his saxophone. We leaned in closer toward the screen.

It was a featurette from the documentary *Alive Inside*, the story of a man with severe Alzheimer's.[21] Henry would become suddenly animated when researchers began playing his favorite music from his past. Though he struggled to remember his daughter in the room, he began raving about his favorite musicians once he heard their music.

One of the researchers asked Henry about his favorite Cab Calloway song, to which he responded by singing, in his deep, baritone voice, "I'll Be Home for Christmas," his eyes lighting up with each verse. The researcher summarized: "So in some sense, Henry is restored to himself; he has remembered who he is, and he's reacquired his identity for a while, through the power of music."

"What does music do to you?" the researcher then asked Henry.

Henry's eyes began to shift around. "It gives me the feeling of love, you know, and romance!" he blurted joyously. "Right now the world needs to come into music, singing—you've got beautiful music here! Beautiful! Lovely! . . . The Lord came to me and made me holy. I'm a holy man! So he gave me these sounds!"

And then Henry started singing, "Rosalie, won't you love me?"

Shana set her phone on the bar and looked at me.

"That one is really close to my heart," she reflected. "My grandmother was in a coma for a month following a ruptured aneurism and had no response to stimuli. Until one day when I sang 'Amazing Grace' by her bedside and she reached up and grabbed my hand."

She broke eye contact and looked at the shelves of liquor behind the bar, as if into an infinite void, then smiled. She checked the time on her phone, jumped out of her seat, and hugged me tight before making her way to the stage.

Jad Abumrad and Shima Oliaee produced a nine-part series about Dolly Parton.[22] In one episode, they explore the rare cultural melting pot formed at Parton's concerts, as Republicans, Democrats, rednecks, transvestites, blacks, whites, straights, gays, immigrants, suburbanites, and pretty much any other identity you can imagine stand next to one another, shoulder to shoulder, singing songs that rose from Dolly's heart into their own.

This oneness in otherness has a psychotherapeutic name that Abumrad refers to as "the third"—a cultural space created when two people come together and commit to seeing one another. Parton's concerts, he says, create the "spiritual architecture" for this cultural third space to arise. Politics and identities fade into the background. It's not that these are unimportant—it's just that they aren't *as* important as the songs baptizing their hearts.

Thin spaces integrate this cultural third space: this connectedness to the other, whether the other is the person who is most different than us, or the other is the true self within we've forgotten. Perhaps this is why the Double Door became something of a church for Shana and me. Church ought to be a place where space is created for people to ask their own questions, go on their own evolutionary journeys, and come alongside others as they engage some of the deepest matters of life. Love, doubts, relationships, messiness. Church ought to let unity guide people further into depth and complexity, where our evolution will occur.

Unfortunately, though, church is mostly a place where people are told what to believe—what's right, what's wrong; who's in, who's out. The great business plan of churches, of media organizations, and of politicians—whether they realize they're doing it or not—is manufacturing certainty. This certainty fosters anxiety or frustration about different ideologies, which makes people more dependent on the church or cable station or politician for answers. And make no mistake, this certainty feels *good*. Having the "answers" is addictive.

But certainty closes us off from the other.

At Evangelical churches I've attended, the certainty is theologically tribal. Christians are in; non-Christians or questioning Christians (have pity on them) are out. Once I began questioning some of that theology—genuinely wrestling with my faith—I felt like my doubts inscribed on me a scarlet letter. At progressive churches I've attended, the certainty is around issues of social justice. Progressives are in; conservatives (have pity on them, or, as they say in the south, "bless their heart") are out. Once I began poking holes in this social justice doctrine or questioning its political origins, I felt like people were seeing a white hood over my head.

In both instances, ironically, I had pushed back only *because* I care so deeply about the church not reflecting our culture wars.

This is why, I think, some choose to return or convert to becoming Catholic. The liturgy and silence of the Mass naturally holds space for people to bring their full selves, with all their complexity.

I think there is a name for this third space in Mass: communion.

Imagine you have entered the church with a noisy mind or burdened heart. Whether you've had a great week or an awful week you dip your hand into the holy water and make the sign of the cross just like everyone else.

After the priest proceeds down the aisle, everyone stands together, prays together, then sits together. Synchronization is already unfolding before the Mass has begun. The readings may affect each person differently, but everyone hears the same texts. The priest's homily is on the same gospel text that all priests this day are reflecting on because they are using the Common Lectionary.

After the Liturgy of the Word, when you have been standing and sitting and kneeling and praying and standing again to pass the same peace back and forth across everyone in the sanctuary, you all arrive at the Liturgy of the Eucharist. The synchronization reaches a crescendo when it is time for each person individually to choose to rise from the pew, one row at a time, and join the line. Just like everyone else, you humble your body to genuflect in the aisle next to the pew and make the sign of the cross.

Now the people, the royal priesthood, proceed down the aisle. In front of you might be a guy who rolled up to church with Trump decor on every window of his truck, and behind you could be a young person who retweets everything from AOC (Congresswoman Alexandria Ocasio-Cortez). Across the aisle from you could be a woman who marches at the Pro Life Rally each year in Washington D.C., and behind her could be a teen who just had an abortion.

All of this natural diversity is flowing into unity because you are all proclaiming that your differences don't own your identity. There is one Eucharist, and in your common identity as beloved of God it is yours to receive.

The Eucharist has lifted you up into *sympathy* as you experience how God came down. The metronomes of heartbeats click in unison to the rhythm of love and sacrifice. Like Henry, you remember who you are.

16

Stop, Look, and Listen

THAT AUTUMN OF THE Double Door's final year, tensions rose throughout the country. Donald Trump rose to the top of the Republican ticket, lifted in part by the mainstream media's shift from truth to outrage, a journalistic trend that has worsened since. Democratic nominee Hillary Clinton called Trump supporters "deplorables," fueling social media's algorithms that reward demonizing, caricaturing, and shaming.

Helicopters hovered above my city condo as hundreds gathered uptown to protest the police killing of yet another unarmed black man, an epidemic I had spent my life culpably ignorant of, having lived most of my life in the insulated suburbs where color-blindness reigned and a post-racial doctrine was absorbed, as if Dr. King's dream had already been fulfilled.

I began to sense that fall, and ever since, our need for a return to listening.

Listening was how Ziad learned that all is music as the Double Door shattered his labels.

Listening, I learned from the Godfather, was vital for hearing improvisation in jazz.

"Do you ever listen closely?" Bouncing Man had kept asking me over and over, his glazed eyes hovering over my soul.

Listening was how Shana had journeyed back to herself, her ears opened at the Double Door Inn to the power of the legendary Charles Hairston.

"Enter and listen," the Double Door Inn's half-century-old invitation beckoned.

Powerful music will change you, if nothing else through re-centering your soul and awakening your heart. But first, you have to listen.

I remember reconnecting with some friends I hadn't seen since my days in the Evangelical camp. Excited by the world that was opening up to me through Christian mysticism and the healing rediscovery of my Catholic roots, I jumped right into it when they asked me what I was learning.

Old tensions of guilt and shame fired right back up again as our spiritual discussion quickly devolved into silly conflict about doctrine. Was there a literal hell. Was homosexuality wrong. What did it mean to affirm the authority of the Bible. What could have been a beautiful exchange of stories foundered on what Richard Rohr calls the sin of religion—failure to move from the level of doctrine to inner experience or transformation.[23] This is especially ironic for a tradition that claims a high view of the inner workings of the Holy Spirit.

But then weeks later I caught myself in the exact same transgression—of all places, in a hot tub at three o'clock in the morning with my then-girlfriend's father. Hours into a deep conversation about religion and faith, we were brining in the chlorine. He and I loved heady, theological conversations, though everyone else thought we were insane, as if a good old-fashioned debate was the equivalent of a brutal gang fight.

But that night, I noticed I had been succumbing to a temptation within to feeling more evolved because he was an Evangelical, for a lack of a better term. On the other side of my own season in Evangelicalism, I had been learning to approach doctrines like original sin or the atonement through a different lens. I caught myself in the act of taking out my new tools to measure what was wrong with what I presumed he believed.

It dawned on me to listen to him instead of critiquing him. Not only had Evangelicalism worked just fine for him, but it had also literally saved his life and given it renewed direction, animating a trajectory of generosity and love, which I was directly experiencing at the lake house that weekend. Mysticism could prove *destructive* for someone who needs more structure. If love can flow out of conservatism as well as progressivism, Evangelicalism—or, yes, sometimes even fundamentalism—as well as mysticism, then as far as evolution is concerned, they can actually help to evolve one another in the tensions of their contradictions.

That evening I became wary of judging Evangelicals the way they notoriously judge the LGBTQ community or "non-believers." That was the same kind of arrogance and certainty that had brought me to a dead end before, and it would do the same thing again if I perpetuated the same energy plastered over with labels for different beliefs.

The only way to "transcend and include," as philosopher Ken Wilber has beautifully noted as core to evolution, is to listen.[24] In this country and in our churches, we've been transmitting instead of transcending, dividing instead of including.

My friend and mentor Fr. Dan Riley once reminded me of the important safety rule to "stop, look, and listen," one of the first lessons our loved ones taught us about how to cross the street. The Double Door helped me reclaim this spiritual practice in a world where I was seemingly standing in the middle of the Interstate.

Only wholeness can engage the fullness of complexity; only health can affirm opposites by integrating them. Sympathy isn't bland agreement; it's unity in diversity.

How can we cultivate curiosity about the uniqueness—the *haecceitas*—of each heart and mind? How can we return to a path of intimate experience with the other, to our own continual conversion?

I'm convinced that listening is our only way back.

I sat at a small table near the sound booth during the Monday Night Allstars' first set. Brisk evenings were upon us. Nights at the Double Door Inn were running thin. My only agenda that evening was to savor every song, to sit and be still, to observe my surroundings and listen to the sounds. When my mind wandered, I came back to my ears. When I began "future-tripping," as *The Shack* author Wm. Paul Young once called it, I returned to my senses, hoping they might open my heart. I was trying to follow St. Romuald's rule, "Realize above all that you are in God's presence, and stand there with the attitude of one who stands before the emperor. Empty yourself completely and sit waiting, content with the grace of God, like the chick who tastes nothing and eats nothing but what his mother gives him."

After the Monday Night Allstars' second set began, in that empty space between the sounds, I saw a stout man, fifty-something with big glasses in a blue-and-white striped shirt, loafers, and suspenders walk through the doors of the Double Door. This was the man who had inspired me when I came there with Dave many years before, the patron whose head bounced around unnaturally to the beat of each song, sliding around on his short neck.

The Man with the Bouncing Head walked confidently across those creaky boards, through that space that was his home and straight to the bar, where he methodically ordered a shot of whiskey and a water from Reid and threw two dollars in the tip jug. He then made his way over to the dance floor and stood next to the first pillar that divided the dance floor from the bar area, the same spot where I'd seen him stand many times, the same spot where I'd seen his head bounce a million times. He stood there with his whiskey shot, grinning in anticipation like a man on his wedding day.

I approached him. (Two beers.)

"I see you here all the time," I said to him, extending my hand.

"I come here every Monday," he grinned widely, the joy lifting his glasses from his nose. "You can't call what I do dancing, but that's what I like to do."

In the House of Rising Sounds

"I like the way you dance," I said.

There was nothing in the world he enjoyed more, he said, than live music. He talked about it as if it were oxygen. He attended two to four live shows in Charlotte per week. Wherever there was good music, he was there, bobbing his head, whiskey shot in hand.

As the Monday Night Allstars took the stage for their second set, I knew it was time for me to honor the sacredness of his space. I thanked him and shook his hand. Then I returned to my seat and watched the Man with the Bouncing Head come alive. I watched his heart take flight. I watched freedom in motion. I watched his listening guide him deeper into presence, into embodiment, into the rising sounds that lifted him into his heaven.

17

Resident of Your Own Country

BEFORE A SHOW ONE Monday, Ziad saw me sitting at a back table behind the sound booth, scribbling in my notebook. He said he wanted to introduce me to someone: the percussionist for the Monday Night Allstars, Jim Brock, the man I'd told years before, "This is the closest thing to church I've experienced," to which he smiled back, "I know."

Jim, sixty-four at the time, sat down across from me. The ravines on his face were deep and defined, making me wonder what droughts and storms and floods had carved them. On stage Jim's glassy eyes and gentle grin were reminiscent of Santa Claus. Up close, however, his face was square and bold and intense. But then he would smile, his eyes sparkling, and I felt I could tell him anything.

Jim's long, white ponytail stretched down the middle of his back. My hair was down to my shoulders. "Those long hairs are like antennas," Jim laughed. "You start cutting those things down and you can't get reception."

Jim told me he started playing the drums when he was ten, and by age eleven he was playing gigs for money. Besides drumming he'd held only two jobs: one when he graduated from high school, which lasted only three months, and another when he moved to Charlotte and couldn't find a gig, which lasted only three weeks.

"Man, it's like I didn't have a choice in it," Jim reflected. "It's like the Big Guy sent down a lightning bolt and said, 'This is what you're gonna do for the rest of your life.' Music has always done it for me. Not saying it's easy, but I've stayed with it. I never wanted to do anything else. It felt good to me in every way I can think of. And it's really not the drums I cared about. It's the music and the role that the drums played."

Jim had helped lay down between five and six hundred recordings. His first show in Charlotte was at the Double Door Inn, of course, and he had been with the Monday Night Allstars since their genesis. "That's one thousand one hundred Mondays," he laughed. I was reminded of a Malcolm Gladwell concept in his book *Outliers*—the theory that it takes ten thousand hours of practice to become an expert in any field. Joe Lindsay, the Allstars' electric guitarist, would later tell me he viewed Monday nights at the Double Door Inn as practice—an opportunity to experiment. When all is music, when all is practice, when all is experimentation, there is nothing to lose and everything to learn.

Jim's favorite projects, he said, were the folk records ("because folk has no rules") and the records with female artists ("because women have always had to fight to get what they want"), which have largely defined his career.

"A lot of people get impatient in this business because they try to be who they admire, and you can't do that," he said. "You can be influenced, but there's only one Springsteen. A lot of female artists aren't like that, but a lot of male artists are—they want to be like their mentor. My career has been all about female artists, man. I'm a little different, and it seems like the female artists dig that."

"What do you mean, different?" I asked.

"Well, I grew up in the years before YouTube," he laughed. "We had something better—record stores. I always had this thing for ethnic music. There are these guys who go out into the Amazon with a microphone and capture sounds. So I kind of came up with my own stuff. I'd take a drum and instead of playing it traditionally, I might flip it on its side and play it another way, trying to mimic that stuff I was hearing. The most important thing a musician can do is to put his own fingerprint on the music in some subtle way. It's almost like I created my own country, but I was the only resident."

Creating your own country, I thought, was what the Double Door Inn had done with its commitment to blues, soul, and jazz in a booming city more concerned with new and shiny than culture and tradition. I thought of creators like Lin-Manuel Miranda, who spent seven years writing a hip-hop musical about Alexander Hamilton, an obscure founding father . . . or Kurt Vonnegut, that great Hoosier who created his own genre that combined satire and science fiction, where the weirdness and absurdity of his stories freed you to become a resident in *his* world. The title of his memoir was fitting, *A Man Without a Country*, for that is often the first step in creating one's own country: to be without one.

Many of our most celebrated projects should have been nearly impossible to pitch in their obscurity. Yet their creators decided to make obscurity their home, not for the sake of standing out, but because that's the home that found them.

I once had a client named Coop who, at fifty years old, dribbled a basketball three thousand miles across the United States (about a marathon per day), stopping at different gymnasiums around the country. When he reached the East Coast, he got on his ElliptiGO and started journeying west, parking his camper at one spot along the route and then riding his bike out and back. If he got a call from SpaceX or Tesla to install more CNC router machines—his line of work—he would pause his journey, fly out to Los Angeles for an installation, then fly back to where he left off on his ElliptiGO ride. Coop told me his goal was to find a sponsor one day so he could truly make dribbling and biking his lifestyle.

I exercise to get it over with. Coop dribbles all day long because it's who he is. I asked him several times during the course of our project why he did what he did. He could never give me a clear answer. It was like asking birds why they fly.

Coop is a latter-day St. Francis of Assisi, who wandered the countryside with his brothers, singing and praying, without agenda, open to every new experience within Creation—person, plant, or beast—for he embraced each encounter as a remnant of divine grace. Coop truly operated that way. He would read people's license plates in a parking lot, find one intriguing, and then strike up a conversation with the driver. Before you knew it, he was giving them a ride on his ElliptiGO and they were inviting him over for dinner. A road sign or billboard in some podunk town would remind him of a loved one, so he would pause his journey and spend the next several hours talking to locals and learning about the town. Next thing you knew, a widow or widower would be confiding in him about the recent death of their spouse, and he'd be getting their loved one's photo to decal on his motorhome.

Many people look at Coop like he is an alien. He is. In this country which operates on timetables and production, I have never seen someone live so freely outside the construct of time or agenda. His life is his own dance, and he finds no need to go looking for a different song. His motorhome, his bike, his running shoes, the different jerseys he wears each day to go along with his Los Angeles Dodgers helmet—these are all elements of his own country. So in touch with who he is and whose he is from cultivating this everyday abbey, it's no surprise, then, that he often becomes a co-creator of thin spaces for others.

Thomas Merton once wrote, "For me to be a saint means to be myself. Therefore the problem of sanctity and salvation is in fact the problem of finding out who I am and of discovering my true self."[25] There's much talk in our culture about being "true to yourself" or being "authentic," but I think it misses Merton's mark. I may have felt like I was being "true to myself" when I argued with my girl-friend's father in the hot tub—you know, taking a stand against Evangelicalism!—but if my beliefs were cloaked in judgment, then I was probably just being an asshole. As Ted Lasso said, "Be curious, not judgmental." Being hellbent on rightness is usually more about ego than the "true self." Forming one's own country with ego as the form of government guarantees its eventual collapse. In a democracy, listening ought to reign. When the dynamic is more about power than people, it becomes totalitarianism.

Although we can't become thin spaces for others when our egos are calling the shots, it doesn't require demonizing the ego. Unchecked ego can drag us down into the false self, but healthy ego can prompt us into authentic action. In my depressive spells, sometimes my ego is what gets me out of bed. The thought of publishing something new gets me at the keyboard again, which gives creativity a chance, which might guide me back to my true self. Creativity has a way of awakening our true selves because we are trusting our own *haecceitas*—our own particularity, how we've been uniquely loved into existence. Creativity helps us to form our own country, just as it did for Jim Brock.

For Coop, that crazy nut, he goes to a creative place when he bounces his basketball. He's not performing. He's not trying to impress anyone. I've heard many marketing people, awed and bewildered by Coop, suggest to him that he document his travels: through live streams, daily posts, vlogs, trackers that update followers on his whereabouts, etc. Coop doesn't care about any of that. Visit his social media. You'll be thoroughly confused. He was once encouraged to get in the Guinness Book of World Records. "Why would I do that?" Coop told me. "God already has my name in the Book of Life."

It's just Coop and God out there on dusty desert roads through Indian Reservations, on noisy city streets, and in rolling Kentucky hills; through grasslands and ghettos; through prairies and university campuses; as he makes his way from coast to coast. I think that's what Merton meant by the true self, what Jim meant by creating one's own country. In finding spaces where we come into contact with how we are already held and carried by the love that formed us, we begin to, as St. Francis said, "make a dwelling-place within ourselves where he can stay, he who is the Lord God almighty, Father, Son, and Holy Spirit."[26] Whether to the steady thump of a basketball or the strokes on a drum, we're on our way. We're becoming saints.

18

Drumbeats and Heartbeats

As JIM BROCK AND I sat talking, more people arrived at the Double Door Inn, the energy brimming, cueing to the Allstars it was almost time. Jim shared one more story, about how and why the drum came to be.

"Before the construct of time," Jim said, "all the two-legged and four-legged souls once gathered around the Father of the Universe. The two-legged souls, being the most curious of all the souls, decided that they would venture into the Land of the Dead—planet Earth—to appease their inquisitiveness. The Father, worried they wouldn't be able to find their way back, sent down the drum so they could communicate back to him."

"That's why drums in a lot of cultures, it's not a musical instrument, it's a vehicle," Jim said. "In native music, the dances and songs are prayers, and the drum carries them up."

Almost every culture throughout human history has utilized the drum in some way, Jim said, creating one global, collective drumbeat. So many cultures. So many languages. So many differences. But through it all, one instrument, one vehicle: a drum.

"And here's the thing, too," Jim added, "everyone comes from the same place: the womb. So when we were submerged in our mothers' water, the sound of her heartbeat must have been deafening. You know that water amplifies sound, right? We don't remember it, but I believe our souls do."

"Is the drum a vehicle for you? Is it prayer for you?" I asked.

"Absolutely," Jim said, "prayers of thanks."

How was I listening? How was I following? How was I returning? I wondered.

There came a time after my move to Charlotte when I was lost in the Land of the Dead, unable to hear the drum calling me home. No matter where I went, it seemed, I always hit a dead-end. I felt as if a veil had been pulled back, revealing the insecurities I had battled for so long as ontological truths. What was being exposed was the fundamental brokenness of my being—an awareness that can only be described, I think, as shame.

But how can you tell shame is a lie when it has become your reality? In betrayal, every lie you ever told yourself is suddenly confirmed through the actions of another as the truth.

I felt like all the inner work I had done no longer mattered—my spiritual reconstruction, the years of therapy, the awareness of the different hallways and rooms of my interior castle, all the curious questioning and the searching in those dark rooms I had long feared to enter. Now "real life" was laying siege to my inner castle, stripping it of hominess and color. The art lining its walls, the shelves of transformative books, the dream-filled journals, the framed snapshots of smiles—all of these were just disguises of the desolate truth now being revealed. The castle was empty, wind whistling through its tattered remnants of memories. It was standing only because of its bare bones; it was no longer a home. Would the bones be brought to life?

Worried sick, Mom suggested to Dad that he fly down to Charlotte. I wasn't eating. Dad took me out. We ate. We drank. That night everything went back to normal. Until the next morning, when he held me as I screamed and flailed about like a man possessed. Another siege at daybreak, though there was nothing left inside the castle to take. I found my home in his arms, as I always had, and in the gentle kisses of my shepherd-beagle, Bailee, who did all she could to hunt down inside whatever had taken hold of me.

Later, my therapist informed me that I'd likely had my first panic attack. Two more would follow.

I returned to Indiana for an extended period of time. I was struck by her simplicity and consistency, the grace in her contentment, the quiet acceptance of who she was, where she was, as she is.

Charlotte always seemed to be navigating some kind of identity crisis, but Indiana sought to be nothing more than herself. Charlotte was always adding another slick high-rise to its skyline, another condo division to its architecture (always more condos). In Indiana I dodged the same potholes on winter-worn country roads; I saw the same cars in the parking lot at the golf course where I worked in high school and college; I waved to the same neighbors as I rattled up the gravel driveway of my parents' ranch house. Mom always had my favorite spicy chicken noodle soup on the stove, and Dad had a new beer in the fridge for us to try. In Indiana the world stopped spinning. Her silent humility invited me in.

Charlotte was always celebrating the next bank merger, lusting after world-class status, chasing a shine that would never suffice—obsessed with her reflection. Indiana seemed to settle more into herself. Boring, perhaps. Old-fashioned, sure. But perfectly at peace, that peace I desperately craved. In Indiana I began to gain what Shana had called an "innocence and acceptance" for myself, as my family reflected Indiana's grace and embrace. The pain did not disappear. In fact, it only seemed to worsen as I relinquished control, but at least I was no longer flung into the sky by a cyclone of inner lies.

Gazing out at the soybean field behind my parents' house, in that freeing openness where I was raised, gripped by the stillness of the country beneath that sheet of stars I had forgotten, brushed by a crisp wind whistling across the cornfield, the smell of nearby pastures lingering in the autumn air—I felt as if there was enough space to hold my chaos.

Maybe my chaos was part of my this-ness, my *haecceitas*, simply because that's how things had unfolded on my own journey. This path was mine, even if it guided me deeper into the nothingness, into the desert. It was up to me to accept it, as Indiana had always accepted me. Indiana reminded me there is no such thing as a dead end when you're surrounded by the expanse of a soybean field. That field became Iguazu. That field became the Double Door. I had seen that field ten thousand times but had I really ever really *looked* at it? Had I ever listened to what it had to say? What is a dead-end but an opportunity to be found again, to unlock another door within that interior castle of Belovedness?

It took a thin space to reacquaint my ears with the drum's gentle call, for me to hear the faint *thump-thump-thump* of my heartbeat again. Sometimes the only option is to return to the place where truth has grown—those well-worn places in our lives where we might walk on fractured ground yet somehow still sense that heaven is near and therefore hope is around the corner. It may be a messy hope, trusting despite evidence to the contrary there are still such things as love and goodness. It may be that our hearts have shifted out of place but we find them beating, still.

Love had sounded for me, and, as Merton wrote, all things now hummed with the resonance of its sounding. It was subtle, faint in the distance, but I knew it to be true.

I listened. I followed. I returned.

I took a step toward home.

19

How and Why

As I was sitting at the bar the Monday after my conversation with Jim Brock, he pulled up a stool next to me before the show, as if to catch up like we were old friends. He told me our conversation the week before had made him think of another story about the call of the drum, the splendor of sound.

"There was this guy I knew growing up," Jim said, "Bob Thompson, a little older than me, a percussionist. He was very unique. He showed me there aren't really any rules to what you do, and he exposed me to all kinds of percussion instruments when I was really young. Also, he had chickens. He would put little bells in the chicken coop, and the chickens would go in at night to roost and start pecking the bells and playing music. One day I said, 'Why do you do that?' He told me, 'Well, I like to hear it, they like to do it, and when they have the bells, they give me more eggs.'"

"So," Jim continued, "he kind of got me into this whole experience of how rhythm fits into the nature of things, which kind of led to, you know, the music of these different cultures who aren't swayed by the radio, and why they do what they do." Then Jim paused and said, "It's almost like it's more important to know *why* you do it than *how* you do it."

I could feel his words sinking into my soul like seeds scattered on a small patch of wet ground in the middle of rocky terrain. My creative life had often been a steady push and pull between those two forces—the why and the how. Though both were necessary, I felt like I too often neglected this *why*, obsessed with cracking *how's* code. I was familiar with that thief in the night who sometimes tried to poison my deepest desires with the aggravating, results-focused "how" questions.

"It seems like a lot of people just gravitate toward the how," I added, wondering if Jim could sense my own struggle. "How to get what they think they want. But the why seems to have a lot more to do with your own personal experience and your own interior journey."

"You'd be surprised by how many people have never been here because they're afraid to walk in," Jim smiled, looking around. "I see people all around this city just trying to get to retirement as quickly and safely as they can. Everybody has to pay their bills, but it's never been what I've been after. It's never been about making a lot of money. The other thing is so much more important: the journey of why."

"Has that been a hard journey for you when you see all these other people caught up in the how?" I asked, knowing how challenging it had been for me, at times, to watch others live a life so different than my own, as they elevated things that were generally more tangible, more linear, and more respected by society than slaving away on obscure books. But there was Jim at sixty-four, retirement the last thing on his mind.

Jim briefly pondered my question, then laughed reflectively as he again referenced the "successful" people caught in the societal trap of commodifying.

"Sorry bastards," Jim said.

"Why do you say that?" I said.

"I feel sorry for them because they aren't showing up for their own life. They are afraid to take the leap. You have to show up, man."

"How do you show up?"

"By being truthful and respectful to the gift."

When I was busy chasing "how" strategies, I once sent a message on social media to Wm. Paul Young, author of the bestselling novel *The Shack*. Maybe *he* could connect me with an agent or publisher since I felt my unpublished memoir was in a similar mystical vein.

For five years I had poured my soul into this project, although the "pouring" often entailed daring to sit at my desk and wrestle with this obscure call, eventually mustering the courage after two hours to write one shitty paragraph. Yet I kept returning to the keyboard, even when I felt lost or discouraged, and I kept trying to partner with Inspiration, even when it left me abandoned in an alleyway, drunk on self-doubt. I'd eventually find my way back home to the keyboard, but it was not always pretty, as I went key to key, door to door, pounding like a madman, desperate for an answer. Messaging Paul was the equivalent of a poor man buying a lottery ticket.

No more than an hour or two later, a guy whose book had sold *twenty million copies* called *me*, someone who couldn't get his own book published. Stunned, I thanked Paul profusely for calling and he responded, "This moment, this conversation with you, is grace. It's part of the grace God has for us today. How can I help?"

I told him about my project and rambled about my publishing woes.

Paul patiently listened, then told me that he wrote *The Shack* without a care in the world whether it got published. He had been on an interesting spiritual journey, and his wife encouraged him to write something for his kids that would show what he now believed. They had little money, so whatever he wrote could be a Christmas gift for his family.

Paul didn't connect me to an agent. He didn't connect me to a publisher. But he helped me get back out there and keep creating. He told me something along the lines of, "We are all in the river of God's affection and favor, but most of us are looking for a boat to climb into or a dock to hold onto." He said that the "grace of the day" does not hinge on things going our way. It's always there if we open our eyes to seeing it.

That week I had been frantically looking for a boat (which would put me in control) or a dock (which would free me from having to surrender to the river's flow) to rescue me, some ego boost to convince myself I was whole and my project was good. I neglected the truth that I was already in the river of ultimate wholeness and goodness, which is grace. I had reached out to Paul, desperate to crack the code of *how*—but Paul invited me into something deeper. He brought me back to my love for writing, the *why*. Creatively speaking, the river's flow is our love for what we are doing, not the results of that love.

So much of what we value in this country is laser-focused on *how*: success, influence, money, belongings, getting from Point A to Point B. Most of us are focused more on wishing for what we don't have than on gratitude for what we do have. Marketing ploys target that lack we feel with suggestions for how it can be filled.

Sometimes my natural tendency to gravitate toward what is lacking stokes my determination, but at its worst it can fuel desperation. The Double Door helped me get back to the depth and beauty of the present moment, where I remembered I was enough. Paul helped remind me that the creative process, too, can be a thin space if I let my *why* guide my process instead of getting hung up on the *how*. That tension between the practical (how do I get this thing that I want?) and the mystical (how can I cultivate the mystery I'm carrying?), that tension between the performative (where's the fruit of my labor?) and the creative (the fruit *is* the womb, holding the deepest parts of ourselves), is its own invitation.

I see the spiritual life as a continual awakening to the reality that I am already in the River. My job is to simply float and flow—to enjoy partnering with the current without obsessing over docks and boats. Within this infinite space of grace authenticity can rise, the home of true creativity, where I suddenly find myself creating *out* of the river that connects us all, not for the manmade (and fantasized) dock or boat down the stream. I am where I am, beautifully absorbed with divine affection and favor, and there's nothing the world has to offer, outside of the river, that can convince me I am any more loved or valued than I already am.

Now I can I begin to, as Jim said, treat my art as prayers of thanks, as a vehicle like the drum to find my rhythm within the whole. I begin by showing up, simply by being truthful and respectful to the gift.

We float. We flow. Hills fade into fields, mountains into plains, coasts into oceans, cities into towns, but even rivers course through deserts. No matter where the river bends, we're still floating in the Source—as poet John O'Donohue wrote, we live "like a river flows, carried by the surprise of its own unfolding."[27]

20

Room of Signatures, House of Stories

MIKE THE BARTENDER TOLD me to swing by to experience the happy-hour crowd before the place closed down. So one day I walked in at mid-afternoon, a most unlikely time.

"Welcome to a totally different Double Door Inn experience," Mike chuckled, cracking open my usual IPA, a most unlikely beer.

"Thanks, looks like it," I said, taking a swig.

The majority of the dozen or so people in the bar, Mike explained, had been coming here for decades. "I want to introduce you to someone," he eventually said, turning toward the end of the bar and hollering.

Next thing I knew I was shaking hands with a man in a cowboy hat likely in his seventies or eighties. "Murph, meet Stephen; Stephen, meet Murph." I quickly learned Murph was a fountain of stories. His low, slow, crackled voice had a way of pulling you into the art that is southern storytelling, where they say half the words with a punchline twice as strong.

I asked him what drew him to the venue and, unlike Ziad the saxophonist's philosophical riffs, Murph paused and simply said, "The women and the beer," then pointed to a spot behind the bar where someone once seduced him one rowdy evening in the seventies. I asked Murph if he was a musician, and he laughed, "I can barely play the stereo."

What did the Double Door mean to him, I asked.

"My doctor doesn't want me to drink, so I tell them I go to 'group therapy' twice a week," he said as he poured his Heineken into a glass and looked around at his "group"—a collection of rugged, blue-collar workers, who walked by every ten minutes or so and teased him.

"He knows more than what he looks like he does," one of them said.

Another bummed a cigarette.

Another nudged him and said, "Murph, I gotta get your number again, I lost all my contacts."

"Well, give me a call," Murph said.

"I can't, I lost all my contacts."

"Don't you write your contacts down?"

"No."

"Here, I'll call you," Murph said, pulling up his name. "It's ringing."

"Murph, that's my old number."

"Oh, okay, well, give me your new number."

The man gave him his number.

"Dammit," said Murph, accidentally exiting out the screen. "Give it to me again."

Group therapy in action, no leader necessary.

I'd learn that Murph had certainly left his mark on the Double Door Inn—and not just because of his, uh, sexual acts. All the woodworking, he told me, was his doing: the soundboard, the four elevated theater seats on the back wall between the bathrooms (which they called the Sky Box), and the deck out back. Soon it would all be gone.

Murph's fondest memories were associated with his best friend, Everett. Everett first invited Murph to the Double Door four decades before, just a couple years after it had opened. Everett had an under-the table agreement with Nick that he could buy his beer for a quarter instead of fifty cents, but Nick eventually noticed that Everett kept buying two beers and giving one to Murph. "Hell, just let Murph get beers for a quarter, too," Nick eventually said. Murph wouldn't tell me whether he still got beers for a quarter.

Murph and Everett were co-conspirators in the party they called life. Their jobs, Murph said, served one purpose: to keep the party going. For years they roomed together across the street from the Double Door, where they would often host house parties after bluegrass performances, as people showed up with a case of PBR in one hand and an instrument in another.

Murph went on and on, telling me stories about the wild things that he and his best friend did at the Double Door. In a rare moment of seriousness, staring at the famous, cursive "The Double Door Inn Est. 1973" sign on the brick behind the stage, Murph told me Everett had died two years before. "I helped him paint that sign," Murph cracked. Then he sighed and said, "I'm going to wear a black armband when they knock this thing down."

In memory of the venue.

In memory of his best friend and the time they shared in that sacred place.

In memory of the iconic sign they painted.

When I left that afternoon, I took a moment to marvel at the sign behind the stage. Painted directly on the brick, there was no way to preserve it. This central symbol would soon be rubble on the ground, bits and pieces of unassembled letters, stripped to a memory. But the stories it signified would live on through the lives of all who had passed through.

We all leave markings on the walls of each other's souls—imprints, signatures, carvings—as we shape and form one another, sometimes for better, sometimes for worse. I think our opportunity is to leave markings that positively define each other, which become their own iconic symbols of the story we co-authored together. We make memories that contribute to the flow of another's trajectory on the river. Even if that symbol is one day met by a bulldozer.

I've learned that the inner work I'm willing to do directly impacts the markings I make, from blissful beginnings to bitter ends to brave begin-agains. One of the biggest lies we buy into is that we are somehow defined by endings—when, in fact, journeying has no end. I stared at the sign and, frustrated with my city for neglecting its history, I saw a fate concealed. But I was simultaneously grateful for the mark it left—that we get to paint icons on each other's souls.

After my sortie with the happy-hour crowd I returned that evening to talk to Joe Lindsay, the forty-eight-old electric guitarist for the Monday Night Allstars. We sat at the bar, each drinking a water. Handsome and brown-skinned, clean-shaven and strait-laced, Joe wore a black newsies cap and a dark button-up shirt. I noticed how he always dressed in neutral colors, as if he never wanted to distract the audience from his most prized possession and gift, his guitar, even though his reputation preceded him.

Joe had toured or collaborated with a long list of legends: R&B greats James Brown, Roy C, and Howard Hewett; jazz stars Ronnie Laws, Brian Simpson and Tom Browne; as well as other multi-dimensional artists like K-C & JoJo, Anthony Hamilton, Calvin Richardson, and Stephanie Mills. Yet you would never have known. Joe had a simplicity about him that should not have surprised me considering how nonchalantly he stood in the back corner of the stage every Monday, stoically shredding on his electric guitar. No need for showmanship if the music was good. He told me he never drank or smoked, though he joked he used to inhale a pack a night on Mondays before local no-smoking laws were passed.

Our conversation at the bar was soon eclipsed by how unexpectedly noisy it was. It was still another half-hour before the Monday Night Allstars would take the stage, but each week the crowds had been growing, especially now in December. When news first broke in the spring about the closing, many expected that someone would come along and save it. Now people were realizing this wasn't going to happen and they had only one month left to experience the Double Door's magic.

"It's hard to hear," Joe said, raising his voice. "Ever been up to the green room before?"

I shook my head no.

"Follow me," he said, rising from his stool.

Joe guided me up a set of fragile stairs tucked on the northeast wall of the Double Door, which curved their way into an attic-like space above the bar and storage room. With each creaking step, I thought I might fall through the slats like in a cartoon. We walked down a hallway with unpainted, boarded walls, littered with hundreds of musicians' signatures, as well as their profanities and provocative drawings, and into the "green room," also covered with wild markings.

Imagine the inscriptions on the back of a stall in your high school bathroom. That was the entire upstairs at the Double Door Inn, which is what you might expect if you gave musicians from the seventies and eighties free rein with a pack of permanent markers. Lots of sketches of male and female genitalia, band stickers and caricatures, political statements and drug references, chaotic scribblings and cryptic messages, among what had to have been hundreds of signatures.

If you were taking a tour, the downstairs of the Double Door Inn was more of a highlight reel—all those black-and-white photographs of legends lining the premises—while the green room held every facet of its history: the legends and the jerks, the heroes and the hotheads, old-timers and one-timers, musicians from near and far. All who graced the space were invited to sign the wall, for whether they realized it or not they were part of its history and indeed helped tell its story. The room had a grungy locker-room feel, reminding me that the magic we witnessed on stage happened in the space between normalcy, where the world spins, and mystery, when time seems suspended while music flows.

We stood in the center of the room, marveling at the markings. "Well, look at that," Joe said quietly, pointing at a big, bold signature. It was the legendary Charles Hairston's. I placed my hand on the black star between his first name and his last. Later in the month, I would revisit the green room with Rick, the legendary Charles Hairston's best friend, and he would point to the same signature and say, "It's the biggest thing in here, and it should be."

Joe and I sat down in a couple of plain fold-out chairs, the only objects in the room. Downstairs we could hear Rick warming up his bass. Perhaps at some point this green room had been more like a lounge, with couches and armchairs, but now its sad emptiness indicated it was already being purged of all its belongings. The death-cycle was in motion. Yet all the stories remained, and there Joe and I sat, surrounded by all those signatures, at the confluence of all those rivers.

There is no such thing as a house that is just a house, a room that is just a room, a wall that is just a wall, a forest that is just a forest, a tree that is just a tree, a stream that is just a stream. These are all Creation's scenes where stories unfold. Matter is alive and active, a magnificent fountain we all stand within, our stories mysteriously intersecting.

As I gazed upon the walls of signatures in the green room with Joe, I thought about how every marking had its own story, like Murph and Everett painting the house sign on the brick behind the stage. It wasn't just white paint and calligraphy, it was something two best friends created together—not unlike a mosaic in a cathedral, telling a story we are each invited to read in our own way.

Bestselling author Angela Duckworth shares a parable I adapt for the boys' and girls' golf teams I coach.[28] My adapted parable for these poor kids, who have for some reason decided to torture themselves with this wretched game, starts with a woman who looks through the living-room window of her rural Indiana home and notices something being built in a large field across the street.

Curious, one day she heads over to the site and asks a worker, "What are you doing?" The worker says, "I'm laying bricks."

Unsatisfied with the answer, she heads out the next day and asks another worker, receiving this response: "I'm constructing a building."

Wanting more details, on a third day she asks yet another worker, "What are you doing?" This time she is told, "I'm building a house—a *home*—for a future family, where loved ones will gather, where meaningful conversations will be shared, where stories will unfold."

The first person, Duckworth says, has a job. The second has a career. The third has a calling.

I think people with callings, let's call them mystics, begin to see the depth of everything, the possible thin-ness in life's most menial tasks. St. Teresa of Avila famously wrote that "the Lord walks among the pots and pans."[29] Brother Lawrence learned how to be a contemplative while working in the kitchen.[30] Laying bricks with one's hands becomes more than a task to complete, a living to make; it becomes a collaborative, creative partnership with Love and Life.

Fr. Dan once introduced me to Thich Nhat Hanh's beautiful passage about "inter-being," where Hanh invites readers into the mystery and depth of a simple piece of paper—how it came from a cloud to the rain to a tree, to the logger to the factory to the writer to the printer and publisher, and so on. "As thin as this sheet of paper is," Hanh wrote, "it contains everything in the universe in it."[31] Matter matters.

Not all thin-ness is euphoric oneness, however. During my third and final breakdown in a series of panic attacks, I remember screaming so loud that it hurt, so piercing that the words cut my throat on the way out as if I was coughing up shards of glass. "You like seeing me like this, don't you?" I screamed, my middle fingers toward the sky, perhaps the most honest prayer I had ever prayed. Self-contained in my bathroom (why is it always a bathroom?), I fell to my knees, curled into a fetal position, and sobbed.

Earlier that day, Dad had sent me a picture of a crucifix. It was within reach, and for some reason there on the cold floor I picked it up. I could not stop looking at it: a God-man strapped to a torture device, his blood sweat and tears falling on that tragic, scandalous day, becoming one with the ground of our world, where he made his home both above and below it, in order to pursue the object of his affection: Creation itself, which included all of humanity. Somehow, it was enough that day.

The San Damiano Cross, a Syriac painting that displays Christ on the Cross both crucified and resurrected, is associated with twelfth-century saints Francis and Clare. I think of it as a symbol containing the architecture of the universe. In Clare's letters to Agnes of Prague she encouraged Agnes to "gaze upon, examine, and contemplate" the mysteries contained within the crucifix. Fr. Dan calls this "Franciscan Lectio," a type of deep reading of the Word beyond words.

Another way to say it, these are the inner movements to unveiling the thin spaces that are already in our midst. You can gaze, examine, and contemplate words on a page or a photo in a frame, but you can also gaze, examine, and contemplate the galaxies within a loved one's eyes; the gentle movement of a branch on a tree; the way your friend throws their head back and laughs; a soft blade of light cutting through absolute darkness; the welling tears of a compassionate listener daring to be still within your grief; a mural in a historic blues venue; a graffitied wall in its upper room.

21

Of Khali and Holy Saturday

IN OUR GREEN ROOM conversation, I asked guitarist Joe Lindsay about his musical journey.

"If I'm making people feel good, I'm happy," he answered.

When I asked him about the emotional tumults of the year, he said softly and matter-of-factly, "The things I need to deal with, I deal with. There's no sense getting upset about stuff. I play music all the time and it makes me happy."

"What holds everything together at the Double Door Inn?" I asked.

"I'd have to say one word: love. Music just transcends all that stuff. Brings people together." He described his vocation. "Music brings love to me, and I spread love, that's it. It feels good, and that's pretty much it. That's my story, and I'm sticking to it."

Joe wasn't being trite. He said everything with a gentle smile, always bringing it back to music and happiness. Still, I wondered what had led him there.

Joe joined the Allstars when he moved to Charlotte in the nineties. He viewed each Monday as "practice"—an opportunity to hone a craft he began when he was fourteen and had been doing full-time since graduating from the prestigious Berklee College of Music in Boston in 1989.

"This place taught me to respect the history," Joe said, looking at the signatures around us, those great constellations in the Double Door's sky. "The Double Door was going for twenty years or so before I even stepped in here, so the majority of the history had already happened. You respect the music, doesn't matter what genre it is. It's twelve notes. To me, it's all music. That's all you have to work with. If you can feel it, it's good."

"And sometimes," I added, "what is felt in a place like this through the music isn't always pleasant." I thought about what James Baldwin wrote about the discomforts of sensuality. Joe excitedly piggybacked off my comment.

"Music makes you *feel*—it can lift you up, it can bring you down," he said. "It's like blues, it makes you happy and sad at the same time. Or, just like a love song, it can make you feel terrible, but it can make you feel hopeful. If you just lost your girl, a little love song will make you think of all the good stuff, but it will also remind you that you just lost someone, and now you're sad. A song can make you feel two different ways. A pop song might make you dance but maybe you're offended by the lyrics. So what do you do? Tough decision." Joe paused, then grinned, "You probably go dance."

"How has music helped you to confront the good and the bad in life?" I asked, still trying to crack through what seemed like Joe's armor. His response fascinates me to this day.

"I'm always playing music in my head," Joe said. "I'm the guy who will go to the gym to work out but won't need an iPod. Because I'm singing something. I'm writing something. I don't listen to the radio. I just hear music all the time. Noise is song to me. I like hearing rhythms. I hear them when I'm walking down the street. You've probably seen tap-dancers. They just hear these rhythms and create."

"Do you feel like a tap dancer?" I asked.

"That's something I've always wanted to do."

What do you do when a contemplative window is obliterated by a wrecking ball? I think you do what Joe said. You tap-dance. You take what you learned from that thin space and use it to form rhythms in the nothingness.

Christianity has a name for this space: Holy Saturday, the liminal interlude between the crucifixion and resurrection when Jesus's followers had to wrestle with what life now meant in the absence of the one they followed. For them, being around Jesus was a thin space, a window, a portal to truth. But in an instant he was gone. What did his life mean? What did his death mean?

Peter Rollins tells a parable about a tribe of Christians who packed their belongings and found a new home one day after Christ's horrific crucifixion. They dedicated their lives to following in the footsteps of Christ—how he loved God and scandalously loved others, especially those who were on the margins of society. The tribe's way of life continued for generations. They had no idea other Christians celebrated Easter, Jesus's resurrection from the dead. Centuries later, a group of Christian missionaries stumbled upon the tribe's settlement and shared with them that Christ had risen.

A great celebration ensued, but the chief of the tribe, with a heavy heart, wandered from the party where he was eventually confronted by one of the missionaries about his sorrow. As Rollins writes, this is what the chief shared with the missionary: "For over three hundred years we have followed the ways taught to us by Christ. We followed his ways faithfully, even though it cost us deeply, and we remained resolute despite the fear that death defeated him."[32]

In the emptiness of Holy Saturday, we choose to follow Love even if death has the final say, even if there is no resolve, even if unknowing reigns, even if we have gone all in and our bet blows up in our face. We get back up and love again, without any hope or promise of victory, because that's what Love does, and that's who we are: agents of Love. To quote Mirabai Starr, "We do not need to be afraid of the emptiness. It is in boundlessness that we see the

Real and recognize it as the face of Love. It is in the groundlessness that we find our way home."[33]

I once belonged to a yoga studio called Khali. In North Indian classical music, the word "khali" is used to describe the empty space between two beats, the very space in which rhythm is born. If you have ever done yoga in a silent room, you might be familiar with the power of emptiness. It can feel like loneliness, but if engaged and embraced, a sense of profound solitude opens through the power of silence. It is just you and your breath, you and your mat, you and your practice. Somehow in this space, detached from the things you're commodifying to convince yourself that you are whole, rhythm rises up.

Without empty space in music, there is only noise. Without empty space on a page, it's impossible to have letters which form words which form stories and ideas. Without empty space between heaven and earth, there is no thin-ness. Without inner silence, there is no awareness for rising sound.

Included in Debby Wallace's book about the Double Door Inn (the only other book about the Double Door I'm aware of) is a beautiful piece of writing from Nick Karres's daughter, Kelly, that reminds me of the power of silence and emptiness: "I remember walking into the Double Door with my father on Saturday mornings with an orangeade from Wad's Soda Shop in my tiny hands. I can still hear the old hardwoods creaking beneath my feet as we walked into the building. Even as a little girl I sensed a distinct connection to things past in that old building. Things that not only existed, but still exist. With its dark shadows, long staircases, and tall ceilings, the house invited my curiosity. As I stood still, the old walls seemed to talk to me, telling me a story. As a young girl this experience made me feel very special, as if someone was telling me a secret I wasn't supposed to hear. . . . The next time you walk into the Double Door, stay quiet and listen to the hardwoods creak beneath your feet. You, too, may be lucky enough to hear those old walls talk."[34]

Over the years, I've been privileged to become dear friends with Br. Paul Quenon, a monk at the Abbey of Gethsemani just south of Louisville, Kentucky. Br. Paul entered the abbey when he was nineteen years old and had Thomas Merton as a spiritual director in the 1950s. He's been gracious enough to share with me his haikus and stories about Merton and take me to Merton's hermitage in the woods, where Merton wrote those words about the rain, "At the moment it is still free, and I am in it. I celebrate its gratuity and its meaninglessness."

For Br. Paul and Merton, the monastery and its grounds were thin spaces—the primary sites of their contemplative journeys. They were also spaces of profound emptiness and solitude. Br. Paul once told me that the spiritual life, as he has experienced it, is all about "growing in our capacity for emptiness." Like Joe's metaphor of a tap-dancer, Br. Paul's words seem to take on new meaning each time I consider them. As emptiness expands, so does one's capacity to be filled through everyday moments of grace: through a lover's kiss, through a poetic line, through a beagle's stride, through the memory of a life will lived, through Creation's soft embrace. Since none of it is owned, it can only be received. Without emptiness, there is no awareness of receiving.

The Desert Fathers and Mothers who willingly ventured into the desert, bothered by the manipulative ways of the world, absurdly *chose* the wilderness because it was fruitless. As Merton wrote, they "believed that the wilderness had been created as supremely valuable in the eyes of God precisely because it had no value to men."[35]

In the desert, there is nothing to exploit. Detached from the marketplace, distanced from cities where we frantically attempt to climb higher, consumed by worldliness (a paradigm Merton calls "unreality"), we are paradoxically pulled into a deeper, spiritual reality, an ultimate reality. That is, if we allow the nothingness of the desert to transform us.

I used to be uncomfortable with silence, solitude, and stillness. I was far more comfortable being busy than being bored, doing rather than being. Now I realize that the empty space is where rhythm and music are formed, wandering and flowing in realms we could never have reached in our linearizing. I think that's what Br. Paul meant by "growing in our capacity for emptiness."

You don't find rhythm when you're in control. You find rhythm when you're out of control, emptied, connected to the loving, frightening mystery holding you and carrying you. Where inner poverty and spiritual abundance collide, awareness of connection grows. Rhythm calls out to the tap-dancers.

22

What Good Are Memories?

BEFORE RETURNING TO INDIANA for Christmas, I swung by happy hour to spend time with Mike the Bartender. I remembered one of my first conversations with Mike, seven months or so before, when I switched stools at jazz night and forgot to move the one I left back to its original place. That's what three beers will do to you, a sloppy mistake.

"You've never worked at a bar before, have ya?" he said later on that night.

"Huh?" I said cluelessly.

"Put your stool up next time," he grunted, walking away.

But now he and I had a rapport, so I asked Mike how he was feeling as the Double Door Inn neared the grave.

It had been a long half-decade, Mike told me. One year before, his wife had passed away. Not long before that, he was diagnosed with colorectal cancer. And following his surgery to remove the cancer, he suffered from complications that resulted in him being rushed to the emergency room in the middle of the night, where doctors drained five liters of fluid from his stomach area. The complications, doctors said, nearly killed him. Mike was hit with two different deductibles at ten thousand dollars apiece. The

Double Door Inn hosted a benefit concert to help him cover his expenses.

"I hate to use the cliche, but it's like family," Mike said. "These people," he choked, holding back tears, "they really take care of their own."

The Double Door Inn always had Mike the Bartender.

And Mike the Bartender always had the Double Door Inn.

"Shit, I went a ton of years without drinking," Mike laughed, "and I think I've made up for it the last couple years."

Mike blew his nose.

"How will this place live on through you?" I asked.

Mike paused, thinking about my question, then said, "I think the freedom and the music and just the love. It keeps my heart beating and tapping my toes. And when you get all these people in here, it's like, f*** the rest of the world. Everyone is in here having a good time, and you forget your troubles. During the music everyone is the same. Doesn't matter what you do. Doesn't matter what you've done. You're here, and you are a part of the community."

"Leaving this place behind is like getting out of high school and everyone is going to a different college. You've got Ziad and all those who have done the Monday night thing for twenty-five years. You've got Bill and jazz on Tuesday. Those on the walls here will be playing somewhere else, but it won't be the same. It's going to be weird. This has never happened to us before. It's one thing to get fired. It's another thing to have the rug pulled out from under you."

I knew anything I could say would fall short of the pain he had navigated that half-decade. He had almost lost his life, then lost his wife, and now he was losing his home and family of thirty-eight years. Mike had trusted me with his story, his pain, and I dared to receive it, to hold it with care.

"I don't really know how to honestly describe it," he continued. "It's starting to well up inside. It's like,—" he paused once more, choking on his words, "it's like you've got all your memories, but at the same time that's all you can have."

As a couple happy-hour regulars walked through the door, Mike switched the subject, wiped his eyes, and began telling me a ridiculous story from the Double Door Inn's drug era known as the seventies. I had heard a similar story from Murph. I again found myself baffled that a place could be so sacred and insane at the same time. The burning bush became a raging firestorm.

Mike began reminiscing with the regulars. I finished my beer, shook his hand, and told him "Merry Christmas." I pushed in my stool.

Like Joe's comments about tap-dancing and forming rhythms in the void, I replayed Mike the Bartender's words in my head: *It's like you've got all your memories, but at the same time that's all you can have.* Mike seemed to capture the messiness of letting go of a thin space and the intensity of grief that might accompany that journey. Mike was losing more than a music venue that had been a contemplative window to him for a few years, as the Double Door was for me. Mike was also losing his vocation, his routine, and, most importantly, the house whose community had helped him through the passing of his wife and his journey through cancer.

There are two kinds of transitions: natural, seasonal transitions and unnatural, trapdoor transitions. Like Mike said, "It's another thing to have the rug pulled out from under you." The seasonal transitions have their challenges but are also as natural as the tide. Many people feel called, at some point or another, to leave a particular job. Many people of faith are familiar with it evolving, carrying them into dead-ends and new lands. It is not unusual to experience resistance in the desert while pursuing a creative call we thought we'd received. Even breakups or separations are painful reminders of what we already know, that starting over is more likely than finding a lifelong partner who will stay by your side. Life is an album of songs—a series of beginnings and endings, of joys and pains, all flowing into one another in what we hope might be a unified whole.

But then there are trapdoor transitions we didn't see coming, those sudden blows when it feels as if the universe or *God* pulled the lever, exposing some random glitch in the system of life. There is nowhere to go and nothing to do but heal, whatever that might mean when our entire world has changed.

This is the path of descent, so familiar to Mike when he lost his wife, one that he might have to venture down again, in a different way, in the loss of the Double Door. I think Mike is right—all we have are memories. These memories will transcend time. Meanwhile, perhaps, the only hope is to sink into the emptiness and to be found somewhere else; to be swallowed by a whale, carried away beneath the surface of the storm, and spit out onto a new land. Perhaps with a new mission, or maybe, like Jonah, the same mission as before, but as a transformed person.

Can moments truly pass us by if we take them with us? Neuroscience has shown that we leave actual imprints on one another's brains and therefore, in a very real way, become a conduit for our loved ones, and those we loved, to live through us and carry us deeper into Love itself. Thin spaces leave their marks on us—they groove new trenches in our minds—and memory helps us to deepen those trenches, to return again and again to the stories that changed us.

23

Serve Somebody

When I had met up with Nick Karres for the first time earlier that spring, he gave me the phone numbers of two of his friends, Tinsley Ellis and Jimmy Thackery (Nighthawks), two veteran musicians and renowned guitarists who had been Double Door Inn staples through the decades. Tinsley and Jimmy, I could tell, were important to Nick. Whenever Nick and I crossed paths at the Double Door Inn that year, he often asked me, "Talk to Tinsley and Jimmy yet?"

"No, not yet," I'd admit.

But as winter swept us to the bitter conclusion of the Double Door Inn, I began to wonder how someone like Tinsley or Jimmy were feeling as time ushered a goodbye. No one was coming to save the Double Door. Its historic ride was almost over.

One morning while home in Indiana for Christmas, as the Double Door barreled toward its final show on January 2, I decided to call Tinsley, the fifty-nine-year-old guitarist whose talents had been praised by the *Los Angeles Times* as "a torrent of dazzling musicianship pitched somewhere between the exhilarating volatility of rock and roll and the melancholic passion of urban blues" and by *Rolling Stone* as "achieving pyrotechnics that rival Beck and Clapton."

"Hey, is this Tinsley?" I asked.

"Yes, it is, who is this?"

"It's Stephen, one of Nick Karres's friends from the Double Door Inn—"

"It's about time you called," he laughed.

I knew from videos that Tinsley had gray, scraggily hair, often pulled back in a ponytail, a bushy-circle beard, and a deep, raspy voice perfect for the blues. He was still performing a couple hundred shows a year. The Double Door Inn, he said, had always been like an "oasis" for him on his long tours, ever since he started playing there in 1979. Whenever he and his band were in Charlotte, they refused to play anywhere but the Double Door.

"When we started playing there, I did blues music at a time when there was no interest in blues at all," Tinsley reflected. "And then in 1984, Stevie Ray Vaughan came along and suddenly everyone was interested in blues. For five years, though, we labored there, playing to small crowds, without anyone in our genre having any success. Stevie Ray held the door open for us, and we all walked through. The Double Door was a place where you could be a steward. It was a blues castle, to serve the genre, throughout times of popularity and unpopularity."

I asked him, "How do you grieve the loss of a place where you've always belonged?"

"I've always poured it into song," he said. "That's how I deal with it. Bob Dylan once said, 'You gotta serve somebody.' Everybody has different ways to serve, and for me it's music. I've probably had a thousand venues close down and it's always been like, 'Ah, that's too bad,'" he said apathetically. "But this one is not business. This one is personal. What I think Dylan was talking about is that some people, when a life-changing event occurs, you pour it into sports or drugs or alcohol or religion. For me, it's music. 'Serve somebody' means that you have to serve the master. And music, the muse, is my master.'"

In the House of Rising Sounds

After calling Tinsley, I decided to call Jimmy Thackery, having no idea if he'd pick up. Jimmy, the gray-haired, clean-shaven, and tattooed co-founder of the Nighthawks, was one of the first to discover the Double Door Inn's magical ability to hold and carry sound.

"Hey, is this Jimmy?" I asked.

"Yeah, who is this?"

"It's Stephen, one of Nick Karres's friends from the Double Door Inn—"

"Ahh, finally, Nick told me about you."

Jimmy, at sixty-three years old, was still playing hundreds of shows each year as well. Viewed by blues aficionados as a king on the electric guitar, Jimmy, too, talked about the Double Door Inn as if it was his castle. "When we walked into the Double Door Inn for the first time in 1976 at the behest of the Dixie Dregs, we said, 'Who the hell booked this?'" Jimmy laughed.

But they fell in love with the place. "The entire group of folks were like visiting relatives that you *wanted* to visit," Jimmy continued. "Even the old guy who cleaned the place up after hours was attached to the building and had lived in the house as a child. He even claimed that his momma bathed him in the wretched old claw-foot bathtub in the green room bathroom. By the time I played my last show at the Double Door, the original 'family' had moved on, one by one, replaced by other new family members several times over. In fifty years of show business, in thousands of clubs, there wasn't another place where something like that happened over the decades."

One of Jimmy's fondest memories of the Double Door Inn was in the late seventies or early eighties—during his one-month vacation from the Nighthawks—while he was filling in for Billy Price in his blues band, when the southeast got nailed with a rare blizzard, dumping seven inches of snow on Charlotte. Jimmy and the band were in Washington D.C. when the blizzard swept through, and their next show was scheduled for the Double Door Inn. Should they cancel the gig or journey through the blizzard?

Jimmy called Nick seeking his advice, and Nick, typically nonchalant, said to Jimmy, "Well, it's snowing, but we've been getting some calls. I don't know, man, I think it'd probably be okay for you to come."

As Jimmy drove through the blizzard from D.C., his bandmates "bitching and moaning the whole way," he had reason to doubt Nick's optimism. It was even worse when they arrived in Charlotte and saw that nearly every establishment was closed, even McDonald's. They arrived at the Double Door and set up their equipment, fully expecting no one but Nick himself to show.

"Well . . . people started coming in and shaking off the snow, kicking their boots, and before we know it, we had a full room," Jimmy reflected. "And we had a blast, a screaming blast. Those were the kind of things that would happen in that place."

Jimmy stressed that it was Nick who cultivated this spirit and positioned the Double Door Inn to become what it became. Having played thousands of venues, Jimmy said he was well-accustomed to the scumbag bar-owners who would try to short them on their rightful pay and the "head-banger rock joints" painted entirely black inside, mirroring the owners' souls.

"This is what I've always said about people who have blues joints: those guys have got to be some of the greatest, most patient guys in the business because everybody who got into the blues-honky-tonk business for the money is a fool; there's no money in it," Jimmy said. "You do it because you like the people, and you like what you do, and you like the music and the folks who play it. I don't know anyone who retired and made a lot of money from the blues and honky-tonk business. Nick probably came out okay, but it wasn't even about the building, it was about the lot. That's the tragic thing about it."

There were just a few memories left to make—the last concert, the following Monday.

24

Rain on the Roof

MY SISTER AND I danced and swayed and moved and grooved and whatever else white people do when they're happy and free. The creaky floors were jam-packed with patrons all the way back to that awful shit-stained bathroom, where I would have gladly listened had we been unable to get in.

The theater seats had been moved around the perimeter to make room—the very start, I suppose, of the Double Door Inn's dismantling. Even the heavens struggled to hide their grief that night, as a cold Carolina rain blanketed the evening, filling the rare stoppage of sound with incessant pattering on the roof. The grief, though, however palpable at times, was bolstered by joy, as the evening felt like some strange combination of a wedding and funeral, a great banquet where people had come from near and far to celebrate a life well lived before death had its way, for the Double Door Inn, as that night proved, had never been more alive.

The Monday Night Allstars rocked the altar, performing a three-hour benediction that sent us deeper into the world, deeper into our own lives. I gazed through that contemplative window one last time, as the sound carried me home, toward the empty core, that space of song and dance and paradox and God. I heard each familiar song as if for the first time,[36] the great invitation of sound, or of anything that stirs our senses, including silence, to receive and savor the gift until a deeper sense of connectivity emerges, freeing us (even if only momentarily) from our attachments, from ourselves.

Lifted by the sounds, I could be unashamedly myself, with my own bouncing head. I was a temple, surrounded by other temples, all of us a reflection of what humanity could be if we left the judgments and labels behind.

In the middle of their set, Ziad quieted the crowd and spoke above the rhythms of rain. "Forty-four years of amazing music," he reflected. "So many legendary people who are in the Rock and Roll Hall of Fame played on this stage. And I can't even begin to express to you what this place means to so many people—audience members, musicians, and Charlotte. The legacy of this place will live on forever, and what we want to do is make sure that the spirit of the Double Door moves forward into the future."

Ziad paused, looked around the crowd, and said, "I'd also like to see if Nick Karres is in the house still. We would be remiss if we did not invite him up to the stage if he would like to say something."

I spotted Nick, standing by the soundboard. He was shyly waving his hands, as if to shoo away Ziad and say to him, "This place, all the nights at the Double Door Inn, have always been about music, not about me."

Someone finally shoved a microphone in his face.

"Thank you to everybody for coming out," Nick said quickly, hardly understandable, "for spending your Monday night with us. We love all of you and thank you very much. And we will all miss each other."

That was all that the legendary Nick Karres had to say.

Each song that evening seemed to have a different surprise or guest appearance. There was the original saxophone player of seventeen years, John Alexander; an alto player, Adrian Crutchfield, who was in the middle of a tour with Lionel Richie; a young, talented saxophonist and pianist, Phillip Howe, whom I had seen before on Jazz Night; one of the first singers for the Allstars who took over after the legendary Charles Hairston passed, Jody Colson; and one of the first people ever to play a show at the Double Door Inn, Lenny Federal, who became a major act at the Double Door music scene. And of course there were the usuals: Ziad on sax, Rick on bass, Joe on electric guitar, Jim on the congas, Chris on drums, and the High Priestess of Sympathy singing and dancing and sweating to honor the legendary Charles Hairston. I thought I saw Bouncing Man and the Man with the Bouncing Head and the Godfather of Charlotte Jazz in the sea of faces, but even if they weren't there I was seeing them anyway.

As the night wound down and the Allstars mentioned they had only a few songs left to play, a sadness began to funnel into the room. For the first time that evening it began to feel like a funeral. The party stood still. People embraced.

Was there more we could have done to save the Double Door? If we had supported it over the years the way we did that night, would it have ever had to close? Had we taken it for granted? Was there someone in one of our "networks" who could have come alongside Nick and helped him save it? All the Double Door ever did was love us—had we loved it back? Had greed and pride and money and development won the fight against authenticity? Had the idolatry of property value silenced the rising sounds? Had external conquest defeated internal truth?

Maybe. But I don't think so. For some reason, it was the Double Door Inn's time to go. And now the great invitation was to take the Double Door with us, to live into its authenticity and help others come alive.

The rain fell harder as the Monday Night Allstars wound down. Then, as the Allstars played their third to last song, "Cold Sweat" by James Brown, I kid you not—and anyone who was on the dance floor that evening can attest to this—the roof began to leak, right there in the center of the dance floor, as if the heavens were bursting through, crossing into our three-dimensional space to mix their tears with ours.

As Love always seems to do when grief meets grief, it was breaking through relentlessly with the fervor of a storm yet the grace of a cleansing rain. As long as Love sang, I was going to listen. If goodbye felt like hell, we could not help but conclude that heaven itself was in our midst, a reminder that all of reality is a thin place because it is thick with the divine.

The yawning emptiness could not be explained, but neither could its gifts be denied. I thought of how Jesus came not to explain suffering, but to enter into it.

The Allstars sang Sly and the Family Stone's "Sing A Simple Song," a beautiful vocal collaboration featuring the voices of Shana, Rick, and Chris, which then moved into another Sly song and a Monday Night Allstar staple, "I Want to Take You Higher," featuring all three voices once more. It was back to partying once again, as the rain invaded.

After the song, as the silence settled back onto the sound of the rain, Ziad took the mic. "There will never be another Double Door," he said. "Let's carry the torch forward, and when the next place comes along with this spirit, let's try to take our spirit there and make it what this was and keep the music alive, just like Nick tried to do for so many years. We love you, Nick. You're the man. God bless all of you. Guys, be safe. Happy New Year."

They burst into "I Want to Take You Higher" once more, as if it was their last night on earth, as if they'd never sing again. When the song ended, I thought they were done, but Ziad announced they had one more surprise: the late legendary Charles Hairston was going to send us out.

An old recording began to play through the speakers: Charles singing Sam Cooke's "A Change Is Gonna Come." I was reminded of a video I once saw of Charles, at this hospital in his gown, singing "Talking Old Soldiers" by Elton John. For Charles it was always about what a song could do for the soul.

Couples slow danced. The Monday Night Allstars hugged one another. People in the crowd embraced. Patrons lined up to thank Nick. I pictured the legendary Charles Hairston making his way through the crowd and singing. "It's been a long, a long time coming," Charles sang, "But I know a change is gonna come."

25

Soul of an Artist

"THE YEAR THAT MUSIC died." That's what CNN called it. Some of the world's best musicians passed away that year, from Prince to David Bowie to Glenn Frey (The Eagles) to Paul Kantner (Jefferson Airplane) to Maurice White (Earth, Wind & Fire) to George Michael—the list goes on. Maybe it was fitting for the Double Door Inn to breathe its final breaths when it did, following a year that saw some of our most iconic artists become saints.

After all, those saints needed a place to play.

Ziad sat across from me at the same Dilworth coffeeshop where we'd run into each other months before.

Several weeks had passed since the rain broke through. The Double Door was an empty house now, Ziad said. The photographs had been auctioned. The iconic outdoor sign above the double doors had been taken down. Next step, the venue would be flattened to the ground.

Ziad had told us that final night in his benediction to carry the torch forward, to take the spirit of the Double Door with us. What did he mean? How could we actually take the spirit of thin spaces we'd experienced into the routines of daily life?

"I've always considered the Double Door an actual artist," Ziad responded. "There will never be another Double Door. You can emulate it all you want, and I'll support it, but there'll never be another place like it. The only thing that separates an artist from another artist is their soul and how they define themselves as an individual. What they have to give the world is different than everybody else. It's about sharing what makes you who you are."

"Same thing for an artist like Sam Cooke or James Brown or Eric Clapton," he went on. "An artist leaves something in the world—a book, an album, the tangible legacy of what you created and who you were. If you're the head of a charitable organization, you leave behind the works it did. The Double Door was a living, breathing entity, and it marked the spot of so much artistic power. They say there are certain places on earth where energy is more heightened, and it was probably one of them."

Thin places, I thought to myself.

"How does someone become an artist, someone who reflects the essence of the Double Door Inn?" I asked.

"When you become an artist, you realize that if you gain financial wealth or stability, you'll be one lucky son of a gun," Ziad laughed. "You can work harder than anyone else, it doesn't matter: you still need luck to attain those things. You don't go into it like that, expecting anything. You have to see yourself as a servant."

"Because if your goal is worldly things, you probably aren't a true artist," I added.

"You accept that you are a servant and you embrace it because it's a refuge from all this nastiness that is corporate," Ziad continued. "It's a privilege for me to live this life, despite the struggles. I can tell anyone, anytime, to go f*** themselves," he laughed.

Artists don't let the systems trying to control their lives define them. They're the ones who do the defining, whatever the cost. Sometimes the cost is final.

I added, "A place that was slowly dying financially gave birth to so many things."

"A lot of people saw the Double Door as this amazing place with all the aspects we described, but a lot of people don't see Nick," Ziad continued. "You have to understand: there's no Double Door Inn without Nick, his brother, Matt, the doorman, Todd, and the bartender, Mike. They gave their life to that place. I think it became a great source of joy—and sometimes the greatest source of joy can be the biggest struggle to keep it going. Business is always about reinventing yourself. But the common thread through it all was that people could strike a match to new musical endeavors on that stage."

Ziad told me that the young pianist, saxophonist, and trumpet player Phillip Howe nudged him the final night at the Double Door about Nick. "Is the owner here?" Phillip asked. "Can I meet him?"

They made their way through the crowd toward the sound board.

"Phillip walked up to Nick with tears in his eyes," Ziad recounted. "He could barely talk. He said, 'Man, I want to thank you. This place made me who I am and is why I am who I am. Being able to come here and play and meet people, it's defined what little career I have so far.' He could barely get the words out. Nick was smiling from ear to ear."

"I have the same story," Ziad said, referring to the night he saw Moose Magic perform in the mid seventies, shifting from a Chick Corea song to a Beatles song, and he realized that life is music and music is life. "As far as defining who I am and pivotal moments, it's the same. That says it all. Think about that. I was his age in the mid to late seventies. I came through there and heard some of the most inspiring music I've ever heard."

I thought about the generational impact of the Double Door. Despite the financial struggles Nick had faced the last two to three decades, it continued to be, as Ziad told me, "an ongoing contribution to the world of music." It continued to be a space for powerful music to thrive and bring people together, no matter how many, no matter how few.

"Considering the progression of music, when you look at the nineties through 2010, that twenty-year span, versus the previous seventeen years when the Double Door opened, that was drastically different—*drastically*—to the point that the Double Door Inn barely survived," Ziad reflected. "They had to make some changes. Book different types of bands. And all that iconic imagery, the pictures on the wall, that all happened before 1990. These were artists who defined their genre. Music was kind of out of the box after those seventeen years, and the next thirty was just trying to keep the Double Door Inn going. It was a struggle for Nick, and God bless him for it. Maybe he was stubborn and just refused to give up. Maybe he knew there was something special there and couldn't bear to let it go."

"You ought to swing by it one last time," Ziad said.

About a month after the rain broke through the roof, I decided it was time.

26

Waking Up

On the last afternoon in January I walked into the legendary venue, now a desolate space with naked walls, nothing more than an old, tumbledown building. A month ago she had been bursting with life—with history, with memories, and more than anything else with music, as if her best days were still ahead of her.

That night the humble house had been overflowing with patrons come to pay their respects. The musical legends in black-and-white photographs had lined the perimeter of the venue, surrounding us like angels, as they always did. We had made them proud that night, honoring the mark they left on the Double Door Inn and the mark the Double Door Inn had left on them. The roof had quaked. The rain had leaked through. Even the gods wanted to find their way into the Double Door Inn one last time.

But now the photographs were gone. Iconic signs: gone. Sound board: gone. Pool table: gone. Seating: gone. Only its shedded skin remained—broken brick, sections of dry wall, random two-by-fours, damage and debris. Everything that had been unique to it was gone (except the bathroom still smelled like elephant dung).

I could almost picture an out-of-town realtor walking in and, unfamiliar with the house's historical significance, simply saying,

"This will take a lot of work." The oldest blues venue east of the Mississippi, stripped to its bones. Would those bones be brought to life? No. They wouldn't. There would be no renovations, no preservation, no re-purposing, no museum, no historical monument. Not even a humble headstone.

Years ago, Wallace's book about the Double Door Inn had made this tribute: "Long-standing watering holes just don't exist in every town anymore, let alone provide music under the same ownership . . . More often than not, these places are spots that people reminisce about, telling tired stories of the place that used to be, before the lot was bought up and turned into a shopping mall. The Double Door is the real thing, and it's still here."

Not anymore.

Mike the Bartender scuttled around—moving, stacking, organizing, occasionally grunting or complaining about something: "I've been working more goddamn hours the last week than I did any week all of last year and making less money, too."

A soft ray of light on that overcast day bled into the darkness of the house. I looked over and saw a stack of angels. Where would they find their home?

Mike showed me a distinct nick in the wall where a guy named Bill had fired his gun one night, and then we sat down on a creaky, wooden bench near the front door.

He looked tired.

"So what's going to be next for you?" I asked.

"I'll take a couple months off," he sighed. "Someone asked me that same question the other day and I said, 'I'm gonna do what I always wanted to do: kill people for money.' She laughed and asked me, 'Who are you going to work for?' I said, 'Bank of America.'"

His joking tone fell away. "It's gonna be a bummer for a lot of people in Charlotte. They're used to the dirty floors. They're used to the surly bartender. They're used to the music maybe starting a little later than planned. They're not used to anything else." He paused again, admitted to me he was beginning to feel queasy, and looked off into the haze of uncertainty, "I don't know if my car will know where to go each day."

As I walked around, I could see only a couple of things remaining that even hinted music venue. Stickers on the mirror behind the bar still said, "Support Your Local Musicians." Upstairs, musicians' signatures and profane drawings were still on the walls. I felt as if I ought to kneel before the big, bold, whimsical signature of the legendary Charles Hairston . . . but one, I was afraid I might fall through the floor slats, and two, I got sidetracked by a sketch of a person near Charles' name with both male and female genitalia. An intricate sketch, it was.

When I returned to the empty darkness downstairs, I noticed a hole in the wall the size of an index card, about waste-high, perhaps a wound in the exterior from where a sign or something had been removed. Sunlight was bleeding through, lighting up the insulation, as if They were again trying to find Their way into the empty space. As if Creation was trying to meet the void, not to fix or explain it, but simply to be with it, lighting up the space as Mike the Bartender said his goodbyes.

I like to think that Creation—a thin space to people since the dawn of time—always finds its way in, if we let it, for it is always large enough to receive what we're carrying. Something of a prayer rose up within me as I gazed upon the splintered light, *May I wake up to the everyday moments where the rain and the light are already bursting through.*

Meditating upon the stars, diving into the unfathomable expanse of the ocean, looking out over a range of mountains—no, they do not explain a single ounce of suffering in the world; but the simple reminder of beauty is enough to stir wonder once more. And somehow it is enough to break open and subtly shine through the thickest and tallest of walls. As Thomas Merton wrote, "the gate of heaven is everywhere."[37]

27

All That Is

I ARRIVED AT NICK's quaint, homely place in Myers Park, where he and his wife, Betty, had lived for over forty years. He welcomed me into his kitchen, where the historic outdoor Double Door Inn sign hung at the head of the table.

Nick poured me a glass of Betty's sweet tea—that liquid cocaine I guzzled when I first moved down to Charlotte five years before but had since traded for much healthier habits like craft beer and pipe smoking and not sleeping.

That day at Nick's house, there on the brink of spring, was the first time we had sat down together one-on-one since we'd had our first conversation at the Double Door Inn the spring before. Nick had emailed me a number of times throughout the year, sometimes with the phone numbers of people he thought I should talk to, other times with YouTube links to "powerful music," and other times with bizarre articles like "Would the government let Jesus cure cancer?" I didn't respond, but the answer was no. Too much profit in healthcare.

As we talked, I could tell Nick was somewhat vulnerable as he began settling into his new reality, perhaps in a state of shock that he no longer had his life's work. Though he had every right to be calloused and bitter toward the city of Charlotte, instead he had a gracious demeanor toward the city that made him who he is and provided a space for his venue to thrive as long as it did. From being pulled along on those winding streets in his father's car listening to "powerful music," to taking a momentous ride on the 1965 Myers Park High School football team that went undefeated and won a state championship as one of the first integrated football teams in the south, to the destiny that found him and led to the most historical blues venue in the southeast, he was who he was because of Charlotte, North Carolina. And so was the Double Door Inn.

"The Double Door, what do I want to call it," Nick fumbled. "What I want to say is that I'm *stuck* in the Double Door." Nick looked at me as if he was confessing to me his own insanity. "The music I listen to is still all Double Door people. I don't broaden my horizon. We had this band from Atlanta called the XL's, and when I was closing up the place and I had a zillion things to go through, I found a couple boxes of cassettes, and I'm into this 'power music' thing, and it's kind of weird . . . but what I like is a powerful song, ya know?"

I did know. Powerful music was all Nick ever talked to me about.

"So, I'm going through my cassettes and I see 'The XL's Live.' My old Toyota still has a cassette thing, and I've been listening to that damn tape for two weeks. And the singer, Bill Sheffield, does a song, 'My Imagination,' and these guys are performers—that's what I like to see. You know when you watch somebody perform and they give it their all?" he sniffled.

Kenosis, I thought to myself.

"I like seeing that, with music. Anyway, they do a song called 'My Imagination.' I mean, I don't know, I'm stuck on that and can't get it out of my car. I know it's slightly moronic. I might be a little bit of a moron because I do this, because I can't get away. I'm stuck, but I like it."

"I don't think you're a moron for being stuck at the Double Door," I told Nick.

He smiled. Betty brought me another sweet tea. The two of them had no idea I had just fallen off the wagon.

"Right before 'My Imagination,'" Nick continued, "Bill Sheffield says, 'Here's a song that one of the guys wrote . . . *we wrote it right in this bar.*'"

"Yeah!" Nick exclaimed, startling me. "That's what I'm talking about!" His voice became strained: "The ideas, the creativity, the things that sprung out of the Double Door Inn—what came from that was our purpose. The bands that were created there, the songs that were created there—it's a lot more than just a music bar. Our purpose was to nurture this music scene. And that's what we did without knowing. We did it because it needed to be done."

Before I left Nick's house that day, I brought up how on the final night the ceiling was leaking and it seemed like incarnation, heaven breaking into the world.

Nick responded by telling me about a New Age author named Jane Roberts, a psychic and trance medium, who channeled a personality named Seth. In the mid seventies Nick got hooked on her books, which gave him some language to explain the spiritual reality he was experiencing, much of which he saw and felt and heard and tasted at the Double Door Inn. He had grown up Greek Orthodox but Seth, through Jane, gave Nick a spiritual container for processing the content of his life.

"It answered so many questions that I had in my mind," Nick said. "Seth says God is 'All That Is.' That's what he calls it."

Upon uttering those three words, "all that is," Nick began to choke up once more, this time even more drastic than when he pictured Charles making his way through the crowd at the Double Door and singing without a microphone.

"Why does that make you emotional?" I asked.

"I just know what it means, or what he means by it," he said. "And 'All That Is,' to me, is the trees, the birds, everything. Us.

We're part of God. We have God in us. So everything has a piece of All That Is."

He described how he and Mike would cut out newspaper obituaries of Double Door patrons and tape them behind the bar, complementing the wall of musicians' photographs. When the rain leaked through the roof on the final night, Nick felt that it was, in some way, all those who had died now re-entering a space that had been so dear to them.

"And I'm still looking for the word," Nick said. "I'm thinking 'soul,' that their *souls* were there that night, but that isn't what I mean—"

"Spirit?" I asked.

"There you go, spirit. The spirits of the people no longer here, I think they were there."

I smiled, wiped my eyes, and shook Nick Karres's hand.

I thought about all the powerful music that arose from one place which was started by one man at one moment in time. I didn't know how I thought about Jane or Seth or mediums. I wasn't sure how I felt about Willie Dixon's spirit coming in with the rain that final night at the Double Door. I wasn't sure how I felt about heaven or resurrection during times of life that felt like hell. But I knew this much: I believe in sound; I believe in powerful music.

Sometimes sound comes in chaos or havoc, in a cacophony or sting of pain, in groans within the circle of life. But mostly, everyday sounds are peaceful: a singing bird in the treetop . . . thundering hooves across an empty plain . . . leaves rustling along a worn hiking path . . . the whisper of snowfall . . . the rise and fall of a passing train blowing its horn . . . the grumbling whine of a lawn mower . . . the chants of a crowd at a sports event . . . bursts of laughter from the apartment above . . . or the percolating music inside an unassuming house: jazz with the Godfather on Tuesday night, or Monday Night with the Allstars, the legendary Charles

Hairston leaving the stage and making his smiling way through the crowd.

If the very nature of the cosmos is to sing and play, then listening and singing and playing can awaken our senses to our inherent connection. A thin place becomes that divine conduit, immersing us in what is already true, transforming us as we become aware and choose to join in.

I wonder, if we could feel and see what we hear . . . would sound catch us up in its rising force like a great mist breathed *up* and *out* of creation *into* our lives, lifting our very souls? Would Love, the undergirding force of all reality, flow into us, through us, permeating every corner of our evolving house whether it's so bursting with life that heaven Herself breaks in, or so stripped down to bones that its silence becomes a microphone for the splendor of its memories?

I backed out of Nick's driveway thinking about *all that is.* I dug through my center console and pulled PM #1 from its cracked case. I lowered my windows and played powerful music down those tunneled streets, allowing the southern air to kiss my face, the music to hold me, the sounds to carry me.

My head bounced along.

I turned up the dial.

Epilogue

WHEN I FIRST STARTED gathering stories during the final year of the Double Door Inn, I thought they would build to the climax in which the city has a great awakening for what it is about to lose. But as we all know, that's not the way life works sometimes. The Double Door Inn was flattened to the ground.

A couple years after it closed, I took my wife (then girlfriend) to a show at the Visulite Theatre, down the street, to watch the Monday Night Allstars back when they were still regularly playing together. After the show, I guided her down Charlottetowne Avenue to point out where it had been.

But when we turned the corner I was disoriented. I knew I hadn't turned the wrong way but it sure felt like it. Now there was a four-story brick building, a new "health and sciences center" for Central Piedmont Community College. At least it wasn't shiny new condos . . . it was *educational*. Still, I couldn't help but think about how many students and faculty would walk through those doors and never know they were on sacred ground.

The city had moved on. I had not. Maybe the health and science building could be a thin space. Did I believe the gate of heaven is everywhere? That strange, tumbledown house taught me I must. Still.

I haven't seen Nick since that time at their house when Betty soused me with sweet tea. But when I learned that Betty passed away, I called him. When I told him how much of an honor it was to meet Betty that day at their house, he choked up like he had every time we spoke.

Bill Hanna, the Godfather of Charlotte Jazz, passed away in January 2021. Ziad began hosting weekly jazz nights at Petra's in Plaza Midwood to honor the Godfather. Shana plays weekly at Smoky Joe's. Chris, who I was unable to interview the year the Double Door closed, died suddenly in January 2023; he was fifty-three. I have not heard from Joe, nor Mike, but I think I'm friends with them on Facebook. I learned through the grapevine that Rick might be ill. I'm sure Jim, the Cherokee drummer, still does not have the word "retirement" in his dictionary. I haven't seen the Man with the Bouncing Head, but I like to think he's still attending concerts each week—his own spiritual discipline—and bouncing along as he does, soaring along the rising sounds.

I often think about Jim's parable of the Maker of the Universe providing a drumbeat so the curious two-legged souls could find their way back home from the Land of the Dead. The other day I told my therapist I have no idea how to get back home—to recover who I once was having experienced the goodness and fullness of *shalom,* of perfect peace, through my mother's life and legacy. How can you get back to a life that will never be the same? When you are carrying the gravity of lament in one hand and the lightness of gratitude in the other, how can you find a new way to walk forward?

The world has moved on. I have not.

Everyone keeps building new things. I keep venturing down the corner, peering down a road I knew, going back to a place that no longer exists. Like Nick, I am stuck on powerful music.

Yet now my ears are trained. I will listen for the sounds, for the *drumbeat*, even if it no longer reverberates through my reality in the same way. I will listen for rhythms I haven't learned to recognize. I will let myself be found by everyday conduits of grace. I will find the next thin space to listen again, to ride the wind, to follow, to return.

Endnotes

1. Dave Hickman's *Closer Than Close* is a wonderful onramp for burnt-out Evangelicals to a more cosmic and contemplative spirituality. Hickman uses scripture and church tradition to show how God is already "closer than close" to us than we can imagine, even without striving and performing.

2. This quote is often attributed to Pierre Teilhard de Chardin, the Jesuit paleontologist and mystic whose posthumous book *The Phenomenon of Man* brilliantly bridged theology with evolution at a time when religion and science were at odds; however, the quote has either been adapted or popularized by leadership gurus like Tony Robbins and Wayne Dyer.

3. Included in *Love Had a Compass* by Robert Lax is one of his seminal poems, "The Circus of the Sun," which stunningly uses his experiences with a traveling circus as a metaphor for the beginnings of Creation.

4. The full quote in *No Man Is An Island* by Thomas Merton is worth meditating upon: "There are some men for whom a tree has no reality until they think of cutting it down, for whom an animal has no value until it enters the slaughterhouse, men who never look at anything until they decide to abuse it and who never even notice what they do not want to destroy. These men can hardly know the silence of love: for their love is the absorption of another person's silence in their own noise. And because they do not know the silence of love, they cannot know the silence of God, Who is Charity, Who cannot destroy what He loves, Who is bound, by His own law of Charity, to give life to all those whom He draws into His own silence."

5.   *The Interior Castle* by St. Teresa of Avila offers a beautiful metaphor for the interior life: an inner castle with rooms and mansions to explore as we awaken more to our union with God. James Finley and Mirabai Starr help make St. Teresa of Avila's work more accessible in their course about *The Interior Castle* through the Center for Action and Contemplation: https://cac.org/online-education/.

6.   Thomas Merton's essay "Rain and the Rhinoceros" was first published in a 1965 issue of *Holiday*. It is also included in *Thomas Merton: Spiritual Master*, a collection of Merton's writings compiled by Lawrence S. Cunningham which helps readers experience Merton's core spiritual insights.

7.   From *How (Not) to Speak of God* by Peter Rollins, a profound book that deconstructs religious certainty and serves as an onramp to Christian mysticism.

8.   Merton, *No Man Is an Island*, 35.

9.   In comedian Joe Rogan's July 2019 interview with Cornel West on "The Joe Rogan Experience," West details the dynamics of "soulful kenosis": https://spoti.fi/3ChjEAE. Rogan, despite his sometimes questionable guests and tendency to entertain conspiracies, models the art of listening in his podcast. This is reflected in his diverse guest list and lengthy three-hour conversations where people frequently (and comfortably) open up to him about their stories and ideas.

10.   Rollins, *How (Not) to Speak of God*, 52.

11.   de Waal, *Living with Contradiction*, 53.

12.   Baldwin, *The Fire Next Time*, 35.

13.   One of my favorite collaboration projects was a book with Fr. Dan Riley, OFM, titled *Franciscan Lectio*. The creative process with Fr. Dan simultaneously served as an opportunity to be mentored by a wise man who has been a friar for over five decades.

14.   Pope Francis's message, "Listening with the ear of the heart" for the 56th world day of social communications (January 24, 2022) invites us into the expansive spiritual discipline of listening: https://bit.ly/3iny6jU.

15.   Merton's beautiful poem about the sacred feminine, "Hagia Sophia," included in *The Collected Poems of Thomas Merton*, reflects St. Bonaventure's notion of "fountain fullness" and the animating force of Wisdom: "There is in all things an inexhaustible sweetness and purity, a silence that is a fount of action and joy. It rises up in word-less gentleness and flows out to me from the unseen roots of all created being, welcoming me tenderly, saluting me with indescribable humility. This is at once my own being, my own nature, and the Gift of my Creator's Thought and Art within me, speaking as Hagia Sophia, speaking as my sister, Wisdom."

16.   Miller, *Blue Like Jazz*, vii.

Endnotes

17. Bell, "Everything is Spiritual," https://bit.ly/3IBFPp3.

18. Inspired by the traditional Buddhist parable of Kisa Gotami, Peter Rollins (producer) and Helen Rollins (director) created a haunting short film called "Allone" which tells the story of a bereaved woman who discovers we are all one in our aloneness. Peter Rollins summarizes: "Finally she realizes that we are all unified in our aloneness. It is this movement that captures something of the Cure in pyrotheology. Where we find ourselves connected to the other by acknowledging how our own lack is reflected in the other and shared by the other." https://peterrollins.com/afl/41/2020.

19. *The SCM Post*, "Interview with Peter Rollins," 14–16. https://bit.ly/3CARAZ4.

20. Guitarte, "Choir Members' Heart Rates Modulate In Unison," https://bit.ly/3ir2866.

21. Rossato-Bennett, "Alive Inside," https://bit.ly/3IDl4cI.

22. Abumrad and Oliaee, *Dolly Parton's America,* https://www.wnycstudios.org/podcasts/dolly-partons-america.

23. In *The Naked Now* and *The Universal Christ*, Richard Rohr, OFM, shows how Christianity, at its core, invites us into an inward, non-dualistic journey that is all about transformation.

24. Wilber, *A Brief History of Everything*, 221.

25. For centuries contemplation was viewed as something reserved for monastics. With the publication of his relatable autobiography *The Seven Storey Mountain,* Merton began making contemplation accessible to laypeople. His book *New Seeds of Contemplation*, from which the quote about being a saint is attributed, is his groundbreaking work on the contemplative life.

26. Bodo, "Holy Quotes from St. Francis of Assisi," https://bit.ly/3QsmoCF.

27. O'Donohue, *Conamara Blues: Poems*, 30.

28. Duckworth, *Grit*, 53.

29. St. Teresa of Avila, *The Way of Perfection*, 258.

30. Brother Lawrence, *The Practice of the Presence of God*, 125.

31. Nhat Hanh, *The Heart of Understanding*, 3–4.

32. Rollins, *How (Not) to Speak of God*, 84–85.

33. In Mirabai Starr's *Wild Mercy,* she beautifully weaves together mystical insight from a wide range of religious traditions to describe the dimensions of Wisdom, showing our need today for the sacred feminine.

34. Wallace, *Home of the Blues*, 103.

Endnotes

35. In *Thoughts in Solitude*, Merton shows how the contemplative life is, in many ways, a journey into the desert. He expands on this notion of emptiness in my personal favorite of Merton's works, *Zen and the Birds of Appetite*, as he explores the intersection of Christian mysticism and Zen Buddhism. Writes Merton: "The 'mind of Christ' as described by St. Paul in Philippians may be theologically worlds apart from the 'mind of Buddha' . . . but the utter 'self-emptying' of Christ—and the self-emptying which makes the disciple one with Christ in *His* kenosis—can be understood and has been understood in a very Zen-like sense as far as psychology and experience are concerned."

36. In his poem "Little Gidding," T.S. Eliot wrote: "We shall not cease from exploration / And the end of all our exploring / Will be to arrive where we started / And know the place for the first time." The poem can be accessed through Columbia University: https://bit.ly/3IiVBox.

37. This sentence concludes Merton's famous passage about his mystical experience at the corner of Fourth and Walnut in downtown Louisville, which can be found in *Thomas Merton: Spiritual Master* and *Conjectures of a Guilty Bystander*. I believe that truly meditating upon this passage and imitating it could help heal the division we are experiencing today: "In Louisville, at the corner of Fourth and Walnut, in the center of the shopping district, I was suddenly overwhelmed with the realization that I loved all these people, that they were mine and I theirs, that we could not be alien to one another even though we were total strangers . . . Then it was as if I suddenly saw the secret beauty of their hearts, the depths of their hearts where neither sin nor desire nor self-knowledge can reach, the core of their reality, the person that each one is in God's eyes. If only they could all see themselves as they really *are*. If only we could see each other that way all the time. There would be no more war, no more hatred, no more cruelty, no more greed . . . I suppose the big problem would be that we would fall down and worship each other."

Bibliography

Abumrad, Jad and Shima Oliaee, podcast hosts. "Dolly Parton's America." https://www.wnycstudios.org/podcasts/dolly-partons-america.

Baldwin, James. *The Fire Next Time*. New York: Random House, 1995.

Bell, Rob, speaker. "Everything is Spiritual (2016 Tour Film)." https://bit.ly/3IBFPp3.

Bodo, Murray. "Holy Quotes from St. Francis of Assisi." https://bit.ly/3Qsm0CF.

Brother Lawrence. *The Practice of the Presence of God*. Eastford, CT: Martino 2016.

de Waal, Esther. *Living with Contradiction: An Introduction to Benedictine Spirituality*. Harrisburg, PA: Morehouse Publishing, 1989.

Duckworth, Angela. *Grit: The Power of Passion and Perseverance*. New York: Scribner, 2016.

Guitarte, Aitor. "Choir Members' Heart Rates Modulate In Unison," https://bit.ly/3ir2866.

Hickman, David. *Closer Than Close: Awakening to the Freedom of Your Union with Christ*. Colorado Springs, CO: NavPress, 2016.

Lax, Robert. *Love Had a Compass: Journals and Poetry*. New York: Grove Press, 2019.

Merton, Thomas, ed. Lawrence S. Cunningham. *Thomas Merton: Spiritual Master*. Mahwah, NJ: Paulist Press, 1992.

Merton, Thomas. *The Collected Poems of Thomas Merton*. New York: New Directions, 1977.

———. *New Seeds of Contemplation*. New York: New Directions, 2007.

———. *No Man Is An Island*. New York: HarperOne, 2002.

———. *Thoughts in Solitude*. New York: Farrar, Straus and Giroux, 1999.

Bibliography

Miller, Donald. *Blue Like Jazz: Nonreligious Thoughts on Christian Spirituality.* Nashville, TN: Thomas Nelson, 2003.

Nhat Hanh, Thich. *The Heart of Understanding: Commentaries on the Prajnaparamita Heart Sutra.* Berkeley, CA: Parallax, 2009.

O'Donohue, John. *Conamara Blues: Poems.* New York: DoubleDay, 2000.

Riley, Dan. *Franciscan Lectio: Reading the World Through the Living Word.* Brewster, MA: Paraclete, 2022.

Rohr, Richard. *The Naked Now: Learning to See as the Mystics See.* New York: Crossroad, 2009.

———. *The Universal Christ: How a Forgotten Reality Can Change Everything We See, Hope For, and Believe.* Colorado Springs, CO: Convergent, 2021.

Rollins, Peter. *How (Not) to Speak of God.* Brewster, MA: Paraclete, 2006.

Starr, Mirabai. *Wild Mercy: Living the Fierce and Tender Wisdom of the Women Mystics.* Boulder, CO: Sounds True, 2019.

Teilhard de Chardin, Pierre. *The Phenomenon of Man.* New York: Harper Perennial, 2008.

Teresa of Avila. *The Interior Castle.* Translated by Mirabai Starr. New York: Riverhead, 2004.

———. *The Way of Perfection: Study Edition.* Translated by Kieran Kavanaugh and Otilio Rodriguez. Washington, DC: ICS, 2000.

Wallace, Debby and Daniel Coston. *Home of the Blues: 35 Years Of the Double Door Inn.* Denver, CO: Outskirts, 2009.

Wilber, Ken. *A Brief History of Everything.* Boulder, CO: Shambhala, 2001.

Rossato-Bennett, Michael. "Alive Inside: A Story Of Music and Memory." https://bit.ly/3IDl4cI.

The SCM Post. "Interview with Peter Rollins." https://bit.ly/3CARAZ4.

CPSIA information can be obtained
at www.ICGtesting.com
Printed in the USA
JSHW011902250423
40671JS00005B/15